# THE COMPLETE
# GOLFER'S
# CATALOG

# THE COMPLETE
# GOLFER'S
# CATALOG

## THE FAMOUS, BEST AND MOST UNUSUAL

### EQUIPMENT, COURSES, BOOKS, VIDEOS AND MORE

#### JOHN STRAVINSKY

PRICE STERN SLOAN
Los Angeles

**A FRIEDMAN GROUP BOOK**

© 1989 by Michael Friedman Publishing Group, Inc.

Published by Price Stern Sloan, Inc.
360 North La Cienega Boulevard, Los Angeles, California 90048

Printed in Singapore

9 8 7 6 5 4 3 2 1

First Printing.

LIBRARY OF CONGRESS CATALOGING–IN–PUBLICATION DATA

Stravinsky, John.
   The complete golfer's catalog / by John Stravinsky.
      p.    cm.
   ISBN 0-89586-743-5
   1. Golf.   I. Title.
  GV965.S876    1989
  796.352'3—dc19         88-31945
                           CIP

*THE COMPLETE GOLFER'S CATALOG*
*The Famous, Best and Most Unusual*
*Equipment, Courses, Books, Videos and More*
was prepared and produced by
Michael Friedman Publishing Group, Inc.
15 West 26th Street
New York, New York 10010

Editor: Tim Frew
Designer: Devorah Levinrad
Art Director: Robert W. Kosturko
Photography Editor: Christopher Bain
Photo Researcher: Daniella Jo Nilva
Production Manager: Karen L. Greenberg

Typeset by B.P.E. Graphics, Inc.
Color separations by South Sea International Press Ltd.
Printed and bound in Singapore

# ACKNOWLEDGMENTS

*I would like to thank the following people and publications, without whose help the writing of this book would not have been possible:*
*Robin McMillan, J.B. Mattes, Vincent Pastena and the entire staff at* Golf Magazine, *Al Barkow at* Golf Illustrated, *Michael Kheighley and Terence McSweeney at* Golf Industry, *The* Sports Illustrated *Library,* Golf Digest *and* The National Golf Foundation.

*The Publisher wishes to thank Paragon Sports Inc., of New York City, for the loan of the equipment featured in the front cover photograph.*

# CONTENTS

*Introduction*
page 8

SECTION I
*Equipment*
page 10

SECTION II
*Courses,*
*Resorts*
*and Clubs*
page 90

SECTION III
*Instruction*
page 146

SECTION IV
*Goofy Golf*
page 174

*Bibliography*
*Index*
page 188

# INTRODUCTION

**P**robably the first woman golfer, Mary Queen of Scots was one of the earliest golf nuts, as well. One of the charges at her trial, which ended with her beheading in 1587, was that she was so indifferent as to the murder of her husband that she played golf in the days following his death

Just three hundred years later, a woman in Louisville, Kentucky, Barbara Owen, nominated her husband, Hugh, for "Golfaholic of the Year," an award given by Golfaholics Anonymous, a Carmel, California, group founded in 1984. Some of Hugh's symptoms were: falling asleep on his wedding night after a full day's golf, playing in snowstorms and being unable to engage in "normal activities" because of sore hands.

Today there are almost twenty million golfers who play the game at least once a year—twice as many as ten years ago. While they aren't all total golf nuts, today's hackers spend almost a collective $8.5 billion annually. In 1987, Mr. Average Golfer spent about $370 a year—half on equipment and half on green fees. Thirty-two percent take a golf vacation every year. Somewhere in this vast middle ground are the millions, the ninety-eight percent who can benefit from this book.

Golf's universal appeal stems largely from the game's extreme diversity of experience. Players of every age, shape, and psyche use clubs of constantly changing design, on ever-differring terrain, to effect a wide variety of results. Today's player is absorbed with what kind of equipment to buy, what courses to play, where to vacation, what kind of lessons to take, even what color or compression balls to use.

The following pages cater to the multifaceted needs of today's golfer. If the informative nature of the material is at times tempered by an all-too-subjective or irreverent approach, please forgive us. We're only trying to stay loose. It is, after all, a wild and nutty world out there in Golfland. Fore!

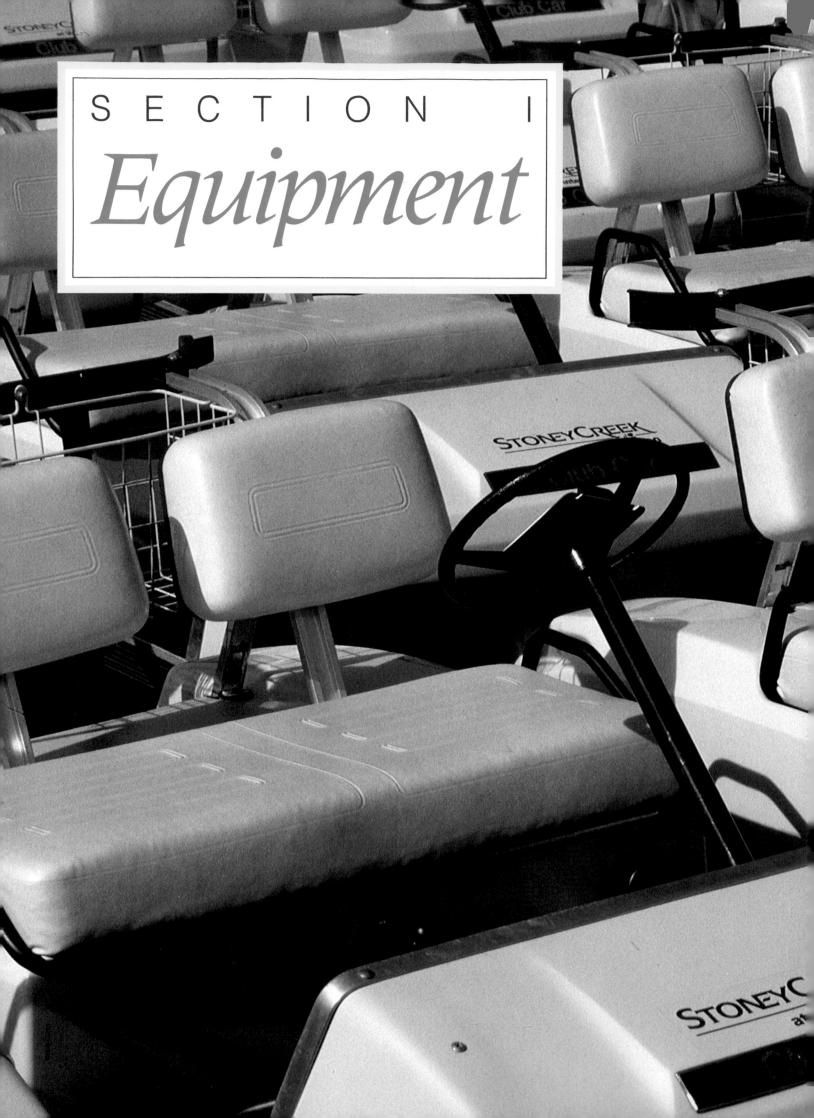

SECTION I

*Equipment*

# IRONS AND WOODS

*"Golf is a game whose aim is to hit a very small ball into an even smaller hole, with weapons, singularly ill-designed for the purpose."*
— Winston Churchill

With all due respect to the great statesman, the hole *is* larger than the ball, even if it does seem smaller—which may sometimes have something to do with one's weapon. Of small comfort to the Prime Minister might have been the fact that golf-club makers have long stayed awake nights trying to improve club design. And they have succeeded, immeasurably. One can only shudder at how difficult the game must have been with the implements available before Sir Winston's time.

The earliest known predecessors to modern golf equipment actually date back to sixteenth-century Scotland, where players first used an assortment of crude homemade clubs, carved in one piece from branches of oak or blackthorn. By 1600, golfers were using shafts glued to heads made of a variety of woods. It would take over two centuries for these mallets to evolve into long, sleek instruments with thin heads—the better to strike the delicate, feathery ball of the day. By 1800, clubmaking had become a craft.

Iron-headed clubs originally appeared in the mid-nineteenth century, although at first they were only used as a last resort to hack a ball out of common bad lies, such as wheel tracks or high grass. You simply didn't dare chop up a ball that took over two hours to make by hand.

But with the arrival of the cheaper, gutta-percha ball, in 1848, golf immediately became a more accessible pastime. This more resilient ball could withstand the hacking from the new "irons," which, thanks to advancing drop-forging methods, were also becoming easier and cheaper to produce. The steel shaft wouldn't replace hickory until the mid-1920s, but, basically, by the turn of the century modern golf-club design had established itself . . . sort of.

From 1920 to 1960, golf-club-making rarely strayed from the classical norm of forged irons and oil-hardened persimmon woods. Top players such as Jones, Hogan and Hagen endorsed their respective equipment, but the differences between brands were minimal. However, in the mid-60s a few daredevil club designers introduced some radical structural changes that, along with a spate of new materials, signaled a revolution in the field. Looks were unimportant; playability was everything. If, some twenty years later, sophisticated technology has appreciably lessened the inherent difficulty in striking the spheroid, you can rest assured that the high-tech quest for help for hackers shows few signs of abating.

Even if at first glance it may not seem like it, what you see today in your local pro shop is still a reasonable facsimile of ye

*Opposite Page:* The great Ben Hogan in his heyday, displaying his stylish follow-through. The classic design of Hogan's golf club line parallels his great career. *Below:* A wood and an iron circa the 1920s—instruments such as these are what led Sir Winston to his cynical view of golf.

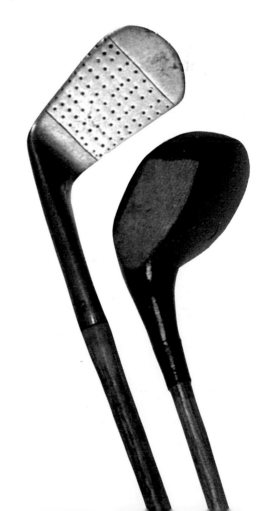

olde spoon or mashie niblick of yesteryear. Don't be put off by words (actually, elements) such as beryllium or titanium, or structural concepts such as compression molding or perimeter weighting. You still have a golf club with a grip, a shaft and a head, fairly unchanged from way back when. The space-age stuff might even help you hit the ball better. And, who knows, perhaps if Winston Churchill had had the occasion to bash a new Surlyn-covered, two-piece ball with a graphite-shafted, cavity-backed, investment-cast 3-iron, he might have felt differently about the suitability of his weaponry.

\* \* \*

The club models selected in the following pages have been chosen for a variety of reasons: traditional value, uniqueness, innovative qualities, popularity, price (high or low) or, as in the case of some of the more outlandish prototypes, just plain wackiness. Essentially, they are the most visible representatives of whatever unique facet they might possess. These clubs are your basic superstars of today's golfing equipment. Some are here because of their historic and traditional appeal, some from computer age development and some simply because they help you hit the ball better—most of the time.

The club head on a Yamaha "wood" is actually made of ceramic-graphite composite. The irons are cavity backed—typical of today's game-improvement clubs.

*Right and Below:*
Ben Hogan's golf
clubs are for
purists. Structural
compromise on
the new Hogan
Apex and Radial
line is too slight to
affect traditional
design. *Opposite
page:* The face
insert and name
on the crown of
Wilson Ultra-Metal
woods help align
club face to
target.

# BEN HOGAN

Ben Hogan's Apex Irons are arguably the most elegant of all golf clubs. These classically forged masterpieces have also traditionally held the reputation of being among the most demanding and unforgiving of clubs. Obviously many hackers don't mind, since they look so good and pros use them so easily. How many people ruined their tennis games trying to hit with that awkward steel contraption that Jimmy Connors used to use so effortlessly?

Actually, the "new" Apexes are more charitably designed than in the past, following a recent industry trend that blends the traditional with the high-tech. The current models have subtly offset club heads, a thicker top line, slightly wider soles and a lower center of gravity—all concessions to the "game-improvement" direction that the Hogan company had previously resisted, at least with respect to their traditional models. However, the current clubs have not compromised their overall look the slightest bit, as seen in the soft, gleaming lines of their high–chrome finish.

The Hogan Radial, a sibling to the Apex, is just as popular a traditional club, if even more exacting. Of some help is the weight distribution in the irons: lower in the long irons to help get the ball up, higher in the short irons for more accuracy.

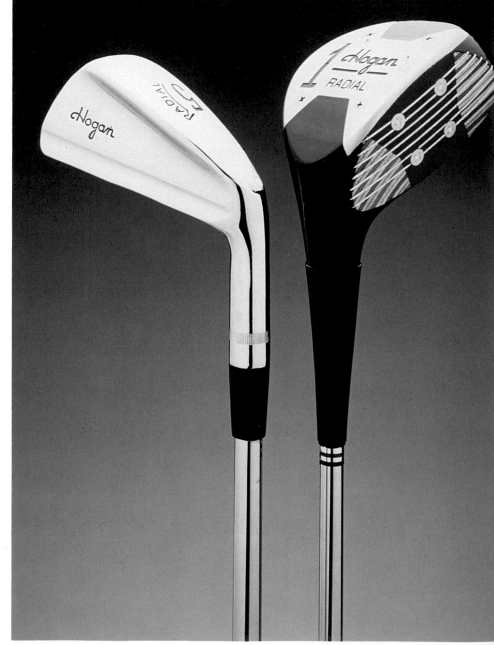

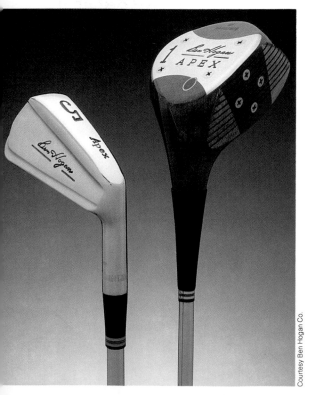

Courtesy Ben Hogan Co.

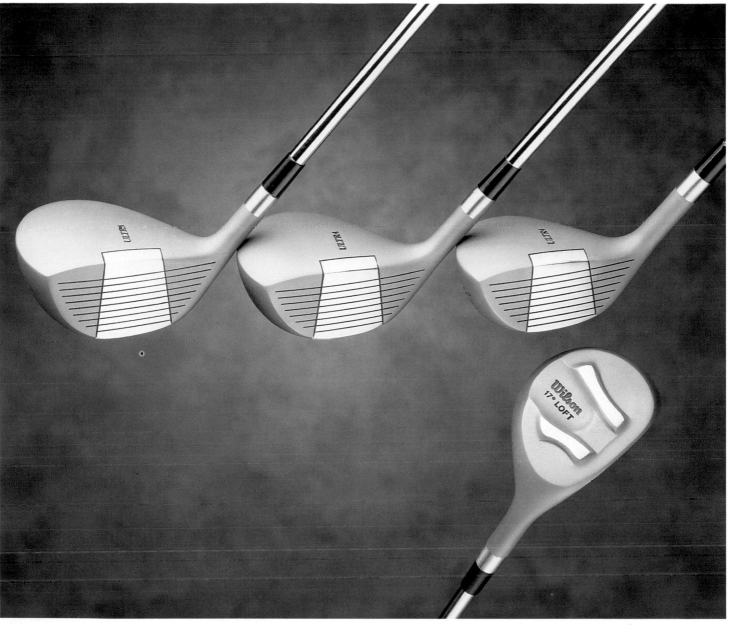

Courtesy Wilson Sporting Goods

# WILSON

Wilson Staff irons have won more tournaments over the past twenty-five years than any other club. One of the reasons that so many professionals play Staffs is the thin top line and straight leading edge that make them among the "cleanest-looking" of the classic, no-frills clubs. (The psychological relief of having a club simply look right at the point of address cannot be discounted, especially among top players.) The traditional muscleback design places the head's weight immediately behind the ball, which allows for controlled power, at least in the hands of the highly skilled.

The idea with Wilson Staffs, as well as with other traditional irons, is to offer a low trajectory hit, resulting in more distance—one staple of the pro game. Sam Snead has been the leading Wilson endorser for over thirty years, which may or may not mean anything. Anyone who's ever seen his swing would agree that even at the age of seventy-five he could probably hit a ball 250 yards straight down the fairway using a kitchen mop. (Wilson's Sam Snead Blue Ridge line is a sensible choice for an inexpensive first set.)

A new Wilson addition is the Staff Gooseneck model, forged to the same standards, but designed for forgiveness in the form of an oversize, perimeter-weighted blade. Also, a slight head-to-toe radius helps with more difficult lies. Again, the blending of the old with the new attempts to try and please everyone, from hackers to pros.

Solid and well-tooled, the hand-finished Tommy Armour driver is virtually unchanged from prized collectibles of the 1950s. This club is made from a hand-selected block of center-grain persimmon.

# TOMMY ARMOUR

In the manner of Rolls-Royces, Martin guitars and other well-tooled precision instruments, Tommy Armour woods do not depreciate. Granted, you buy golf clubs for playability, not for investment, but it's the classic design of these woods that makes them so playable for serious golfers. The current Silver Scot 986 line is vitually unchanged from the Tommy Armour prized collectibles of the 1940s and 1950s (made by MacGregor at the time). These are beautiful, solid clubs.

The traditionally styled Tommy Armour woods are hand-finished and fashioned from a hand-selected block of center-grain persimmon. The standard pear-shape design has proven to be the most structurally reliable in drivers over the years and has often been copied, even in some of the newer, high-tech models. If the 986's substantial club head is for some reason not copious enough, the Silver Scot "Deep Face" driver may be desired. This will provide a fatter club and an overall larger striking area for those who like to carry a big stick (and not swing softly).

By the way, Tommy Armour never designed a golf club in his life. The popular golfer merely lent his name (and nickname—Silver Scot) to sticks actually designed by premier clubmaker Toney Penna.

## CLUB FITTING

Off-the-rack suits can easily cost five hundred dollars—why buy one that doesn't fit? The same holds true for golf clubs. More and more complete sets offer tailoring possibilities that will suit both size requirements and swing dynamics. Here are some important variables (see also "Shafts," p. 28) to consider with the help of a golf pro:

**GRIP SIZE**—If too small, can result in the club turning in your hands, or can cause you to grip too hard. If too large, can hinder proper wrist action.

**SWING WEIGHT**—the weight distribution of a club around a fixed fulcrum point. Should be keyed according to a club's shaft flex and length.

**LIE ANGLE**—the angle formed by the club head and the shaft. Can vary from flat to upright, but should, with fitting, insure that the club lies properly on the ground for the most square contact.

**CLUB LENGTH**—the measurement from the heel of the sole to the top of the grip. Club length should depend as much on ability (usually longer for skilled golfers) as on a golfer's height and arm length.

When paying four- to five-hundred dollars for a complete set of clubs on today's market, one or more of the above specifications is usually featured by the top manufacturers. For those who desire (and can afford) the ultimate fit, a "custom" clubmaker will piece together a personal set from selected components.

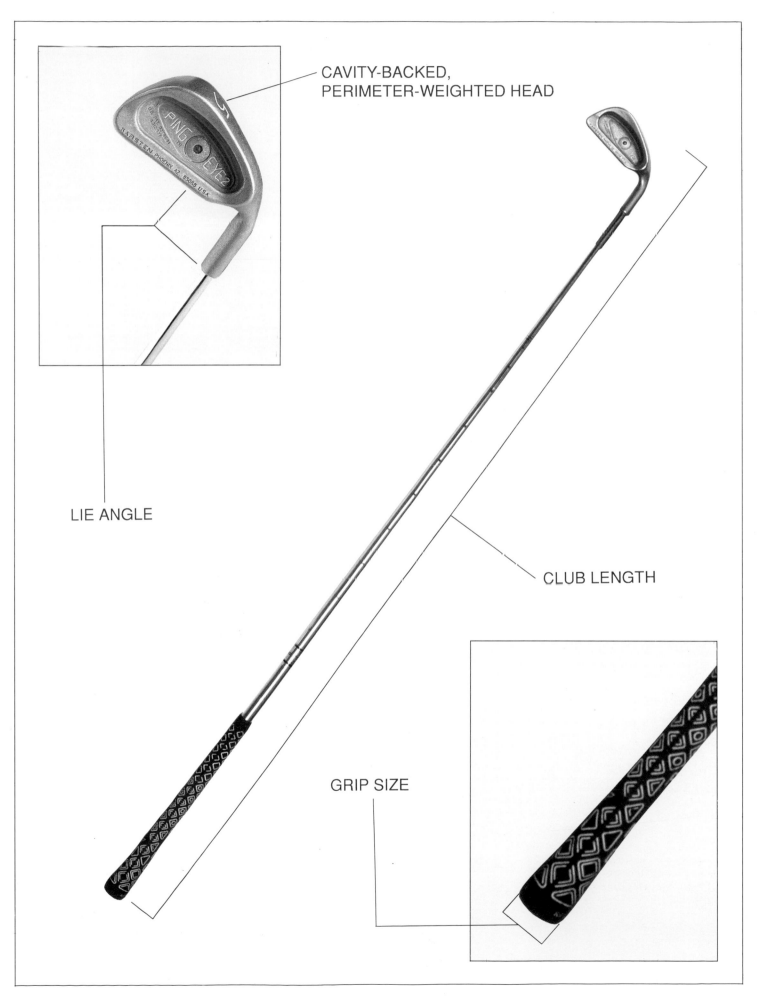

CAVITY-BACKED,
PERIMETER-WEIGHTED HEAD

LIE ANGLE

CLUB LENGTH

GRIP SIZE

The Spalding Executive XE is a low-profile, hollow-backed set that is designed to meet the needs of the "average" golfer. This is a fully integrated set of clubs, with no drastic changes from woods to irons.

## TAYLOR MADE

Not so long ago, all woods and drivers, just like all baseball bats and tennis rackets, were made out of wood. Maybe that's why they were called woods. Now, in one of the more startling oxymoronic twists of modern sports-equipment language, the golfing industry has given us "metal" woods.

Gary Adams of the Taylor Made Company developed the metal wood club in 1979 after statistics showed that iron clubs striking the new two-piece ball (see Balls page 50) were resulting in more distance. Consumers were naturally reticent at first, but once the metal driver caught on with pros such as Lee Trevino, overnight success was virtually guaranteed. Today, over half of the U.S. Open field uses metal woods and nearly every company produces them, with Taylor Made still leading the field.

Conceptually close to the modern investment-cast irons, metal woods are weighted around the club head's extremities, again assuring forgiving mis-hits. (Club manufacturers go to great lengths to tell you about how you can all but miss the entire ball when swinging their club, and that it will still travel 250 yards down the middle of the fairway. Don't believe them.)

Taylor Made offers an interesting array of nineteen loft differentials on their metal woods to fit individual playing styles. A professional might use an exacting 7.0- or 8.5-degree loft driver for extra distance, while weaker players might need as much as twenty to twenty-five degrees to get the ball up in the air. Also, the Taylor clubs feature "tri-dimensional" weighting, an accuracy-seeking concept that balances the club head along three axles: heel-toe, top-bottom and front-back.

Metal woods would be completely hollow if it wasn't for their foam interiors. This is to keep them from ringing like bells when they strike the golf balls. The type and density of foam used can significantly alter the sound, even so much as to approximate that of real wood. But while many competitors have managed to create an actual "thunk" sound, Taylor prefers to retain their distinctive "clink."

Courtesy Austad's

# SPALDING

Not unlike car manufacturers, golf-club makers are forever grasping at straws for anything approaching breakthrough status that might grab the consumer: perimeter-weighted, low-profile-perimeter-weighted, copper-faced-low-profile-perimeter-weighted, graphite-shafted-copper-faced-low-profile-perimeter-weighted, and on, and on and on. Throw in the kitchen sink. More often than not they're forced to come out with lines that are nothing but slightly altered rip-offs of a competitor's innovation. But sometimes a company sticks its neck out just to come up with something completely different—anything. Such is the case with Spalding's Executive XE and Cannon Advance lines. They're slick-looking clubs, they're different, they make sense and they may survive. The verdict is still out.

The Executive XE set is unabashedly designed for what is charitably called the "high-handicap" golfer (high-handicap being an increasingly used general wastebasket term for all out-and-out duffers). The concept is a "fully integrated" eleven-piece set, rather than the traditional three woods/eight irons separation. In other words, here the usually drastic transition from woods to irons is negligible—a continuous metallic flow (stainless steel or silver-laminated woods) from driver to sand wedge. The woods look like irons; the irons look like woods. Call this the unisex club.

The Executive is a low-profile, hollow golf club that blends a lower center of gravity with advanced perimeter-weighting to all but insure that a player, *any player,* will get the ball up in the air quickly for increased carry.

Similar in design and concept to the Executive XE is Spalding's Cannon Advance golf set. The main difference is in the cavity-backed irons: Here, the long irons (two to six) are rear-weighted for accuracy, while the short irons (seven to wedge) return to conventional wide-soled club-head shape. The theory is that longer clubs are more difficult to hit, thus requiring a more compensating design than short irons. The Cannon is sold only in complete sets, bad news for habitual club-losers.

## SHAFTS

The shaft is easily the most under-rated and overlooked component of the golf club. Many golfers make the mistake of routinely switching to a vastly different type of golf club, while paying little or no attention to the type of shaft they use. As any professional or teaching pro knows, the right shaft can make a huge difference in your game.

The most important aspect of a shaft is its degree of flexibility. During the swing, a shaft will bend proportionally to the club-head speed generated, affecting impact. The idea is for the shaft to be as close to straight as possible at impact. Generally the rule of thumb is: stiffer shafts for stronger players; whippier shafts for weaker players. If a player is hitting too many low shots, or pushing or slicing the ball, his shaft may be too stiff. Conversely, if a player is pulling or hooking the ball or hitting too many high shots, he may need a stiffer shaft.

Another consideration is flex distribution. Better golfers prefer a higher flex distribution, because the shortened distance between the hands and the "flexpoint" (where bend occurs) increases control. Lesser-skilled players perform better with a lower bend in the shaft, since this produces higher trajectories, helping to get the ball in the air.

About shaft weight: Light is might; the lighter the shaft, the less work for the club head.

©Carl M. Purcell 1988

Boron, graphite and titanium are some of the newer materials used for shaft construction. Note the importance of the shaft action in the golfer's swing, above. *Below left:* A club maker measures a shaft's swing weight.

*Below:* A club-rack display highlights old and new shafts. *Opposite page:* The legendary Bobby Jones never switched from wooden-shafted clubs, leading many to speculate how much more phenomenal his game would have been with today's equipment.

## CALLAWAY HICKORY STICK

The main reason that steel shafts began replacing hickory in the 1920s was that they weren't as prone to excessive twist, making it easier to control the ball. In fact, the point hammered home repeatedly throughout these pages is that most equipment becomes obsolete as newer models display improved playability. The great Bobby Jones didn't care; he continued to use hickory shafts until he retired in 1930 after winning the Grand Slam (the last golfer to do so). Well, the only differences between Jones and the average golfer were his pluperfect balance, his uncanny ability to repeatedly hit the ball on the sweet spot of the club head and the technically precise, graceful, easy rhythm to his swing. That's all. But for the rest of the golfing world, steel shafts spelled R-E-L-I-E-F.

The Callaway Hickory Stick collection is an attempted return to the grandeur and class of the Bobby Jones era. (They pay plenty for the right to use the late master's name.) These are good-looking golf clubs, even if they do appear to belong under glass museum cases. Actually, they're not fragile at all, especially with the steel core that runs through the center of each hickory shaft. And that's the kicker to this relatively new (1981) club: The steel core eliminates the undersirable torque that resulted from the old hickories. Yet, at the same time, the outside dowel gives great "feel" at impact, due to the highly resilient shock-absorbing qualities of hickory.

In what has to be one of the cheekier pitches of modern-day club sells, the Callaway people recommend that a swing with a "smooth, easy tempo—like that of Bobby Jones" be used for the greatest benefit from their shafts. This is indeed good advice for using any equipment. Is there a clubmaker anywhere who suggests swinging "wild and hard?"

SELKIRK COLLEGE

Learning Resource Centre

NELSON CAMPUS

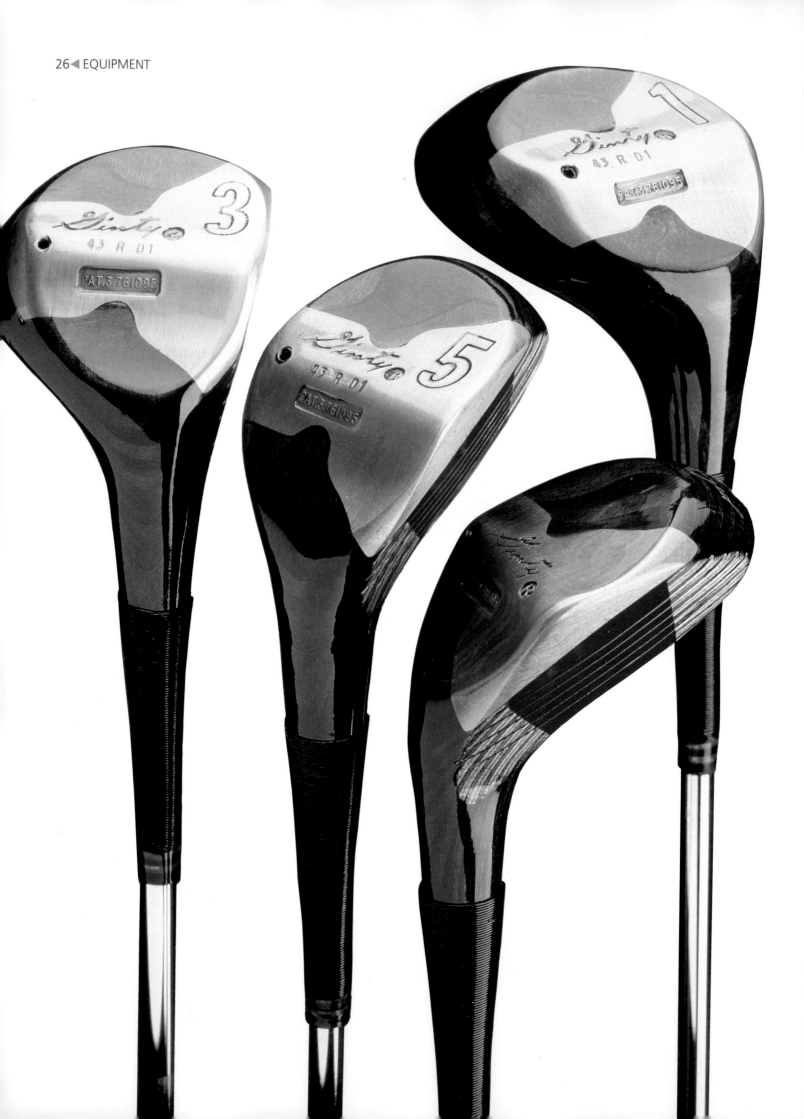

# STAN THOMPSON

*"Golf clubs are like aspirin. You can make them round or you can make them square, but they still have one basic job to perform."* —*Stan Thompson, clubmaker.*

In 1937, Stan Thompson began making custom golf clubs for the Hollywood elite in a little shop in Beverly Hills. Over the years, his business flourished and grew as he made clubs in the traditional mode. But it was the successful development in the early 1970s of the golf world's most well-known "trouble" club, the Ginty, that truly established his company's reputation.

The original Ginty was a fairway wood with an added metal sole plate in the shape of a ship's keel. The club was ideal for use in heavy grass, with the keel spreading the thick grass to pick out the ball in a tight lie. The concept was so popular that Thompson came out with an entire line of Ginty woods in 1979 and irons in 1984. A graphite Ginty is available today, as well. While you may not find the club in every golf pro's bag, the Ginty is a must for the unfortunate many who regularly visit the heavy rough.

©Patrick Ward/Wheeler Pictures

*Opposite page:* The unique keel-shaped metal sole plate of the Stan Thompson Ginty has helped many a hacker out of the rough. *Left:* Today's caddies can thank the maximum fourteen-clubs rule for lightened loads.

## FOURTEEN-CLUB RULE

The fourteen-club-limit rule, rarely observed on any level of play save tournaments, is hardly a picayune one. Imposed by the U.S.G.A. in 1937, the rule came about from the increased and unlimited number of clubs being used at the time. Some professionals had carried, or, rather, their caddies had carried, up to thirty clubs, including spares!

The principle reasons given by the ruling body for the change were: (1) to give caddies relief from unreasonable burdens, (2) to reduce delays resulting from trying to decide which club to use and (3) to give players unable to afford an unlimited supply of clubs an equal opportunity.

In addition, it was generally agreed that the limit would restore the rapidly disappearing demand on shotmaking skills. As one august member of the executive committee put it, "Players should not buy their shots out of the professional's shop but should develop their own skills."

*Above:* Cross-section shows "hollow" clubs: perimeter-weighted iron and foam-filled wood. *Above right:* Colonel Alan B. Shepard, Jr., the man who hit the longest golf shot in history. *Far right:* The "moon club," as displayed at the U.S.G.A. Golf House museum, Far Hills, New Jersey.

# NORTHWESTERN

It's ironic that Northwestern Golf, far and away the leading manufacturer in sheer number of golf clubs, has for years been stigmatized within the industry as a "low-line" producer. They virtually own the beginner's market—their only problem has been getting consumers to return for a second or third set. But with a one-million-stick inventory that turns over three times a year, Northwestern hardly has time to worry about their reputation. They're crying all the way to the bank.

Back in the days of the Depression, one of the company's more clever innovations was the "starter set": fewer clubs in a smaller bag, making it more affordable for people to take up the game.

These days, Northwestern makes just about every kind of club under the sun. If you're looking for a reasonably priced set to meet any particular specifications you might desire—graphite woods, hollow irons, whatever—the Northwestern displays might be as good a place to start looking as any.

The recent Gary Player and Nancy Lopez lines have gained the company added prestige, but among Northwestern's more unique models are the Tom Weiskopf stainless steel "hollow" woods and irons. Hollow clubs provide total perimeter-weighting, resulting in a softer "feel." (This feel business is a tough one, since the ball remains on the club head a grand total of about 1/3000th of a second during impact. However, all golfers will agree that you'll know it when it's right.) Off-center hits might not give resounding accuracy—hey, when they do, we'll know that game-improvement technology has gone too far—but they will afford some compensation. In other words, maybe your slice will be corrected just enough to stay inbounds.

Courtesy/ NASA

## MOON CLUB

One great step for mankind or the longest 6-iron shot in history? When astronaut Alan B. Shepard, Jr., stepped out from his lunar module and hit the famous golf shot on the moon (he actually swung twice—hampered by his backpack, he whiffed on the first try), he left few doubts as to the maniacally obsessive nature of the game. But what most golf nuts around the world were wondering was: What kind of club did he use?

The moon club was made of an ordinary 6-iron head connected by a short steel extension to a multi-sectioned aluminum shaft with Teflon joints. The club was similar to the versatile tool used to scoop soil and rocks from the moon's surface The special heat-resistant ball traveled over one thousand lighter-gravity yards, was never found and is presumably still up there. The club is currently on display in the U.S.G.A. Golf House in Far Hills, New Jersey.

Courtesy USGA Golf House

# MACGREGOR

It should come as no surprise that the greatest player ever to swing a club designs his own weapons. Jack Nicklaus has never been one to leave his fate in the hands of others—witness his charging, near-impossible 1986 Masters victory at the age of forty-six. It also shouldn't surprise that the Golden Bear owns twenty-five percent of MacGregor Golf. The relationship has been long and harmonious, and, at this point, what golf company wouldn't want him in for at least a quarter of the action? A pleasant surprise is the affordability of the Bear's personal stock. But caveat emptor—these are professional tools.

MacGregor's Nicklaus Muirfield 20th line was created for tournament players, which shouldn't scare anyone interested in classic clubs. The woods are dark, oil-hardened persimmon with traditional Eye-O-Matic plastic inserts (for proper set-up); the irons are of forged carbon steel, with the weight high on the blade (for better control among true hitters). Nicklaus has modified the underside with a slight roll from heel to toe for adaptability to uneven lies, but basically you need to hit dead center with these clubs. There is one thing that cannot be denied about the Muirfields: They work for Jack Nicklaus.

In the other direction, MacGregor's computer-designed RPM line is among the latest in game-improvement clubs. The RPMs also cost about twice as much as the Muirfields. (Investment-cast clubs are generally more expensive than forged clubs, as the process is much costlier.) Cast in manganese bronze (softer than stainless steel), the club heads have progressively adjusted blade lengths—the theory being that what's right for one iron isn't right for another. Also introduced is a new concept called "flow-weighting." The center of mass or weight in the club head will move around progressively through a set—out toward the toe on the long irons, then back toward the heel on the shorter irons. All right, so the more expensive RPMs may be easier to play than the Muirfields; they're also shorter on prestige.

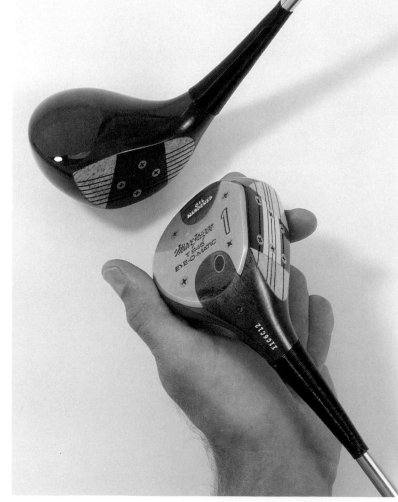

Courtesy MacGregor Golf Products

*Below left:* The Eye-O-Matic insert is a MacGregor standard, intended to help alignment by contrasting and defining the ball at address. Clubs from the Nicklaus dynasty include game improvement, metal woods (*above*) and the Muirfield "20th" (*below*), for scratch golfers.

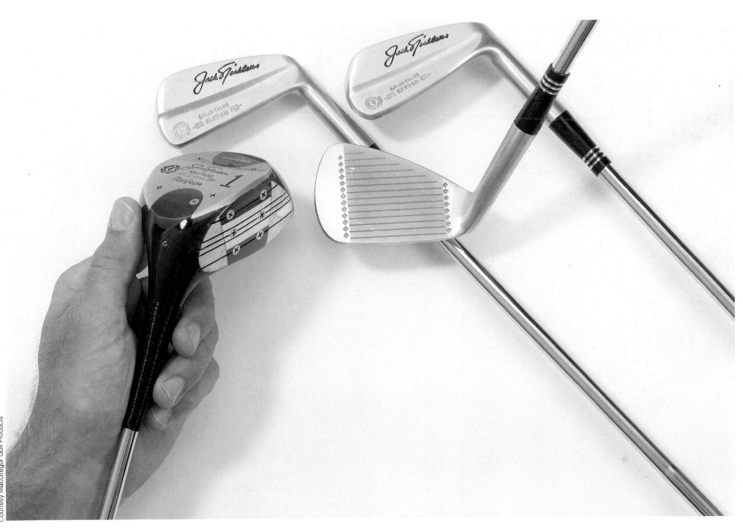

The Ping irons revolutionized the golf industry with their radical design. This design has been so popular that many other companies have followed suit with their own lines of similarly designed irons and woods. Karsten Solheim, patriarch of the Ping dynasty, grew his goatee to cover an old scar.

## PING (Karsten Manufacturing)

It's no small irony that the most popular golf club in the world today is hardly the sleekest. When Karsten Solheim, a mechanical engineer and recreational golfer, began producing his revolutionary Pings in the 1960s, he knew and cared little about a club's looks, devoting all his efforts toward functional design. By molding and casting (rather than forging) irons, Solheim found that he could predominantly weight the club head in the heel and toe, in effect widening the sweet spot. The large and ungainly, humbacked club heads suited his weight-distribution designs and the dull grey finish cut the glare.

Through the then innovative investment-casting method, Solheim eventually expanded the heel-toe concept to perimeter-weighting, which placed the center of gravity *directly behind* where club should meet ball. The result was less rotational twist and more solid hits, even with off-center strikes.

This birth of the "game-improvement" clubs signaled a rash of imitators in the seventies (just about every major club manufacturer currently features a perimeter-weighted line—some are carbon copies of Pings), but to date, Ping remains the most successful. With its extra large club face and hitting area, today's Ping iron is in a sense often compared to the oversize Prince tennis racquet in terms of its "compensating features."

Ping also offers a color-coding system by which clubs are custom-fitted according to a player's height, build and grip size. The standard Ping "Eye 2" irons come in two variations—stainless steel and beryllium cooper, the latter a recent concession to cosmetic demands. The copper even tends to darken with age for an antique look; though Solheim stresses that he's really after the metal's softer feel. And if they feel right, they'll look even better, and so will you.

## YONEX

How much would you like to spend on equipment? Five hundred dollars? One thousand dollars? In Japan, where initiation fees to exclusive country clubs can cost more than an oceanfront villa on the French Riviera (see Courses), a few grand for a new set of sticks is just a drop in the bucket.

In all fairness to Yonex, the Japanese makers of the most expensive clubs on the planet (gold-plated, sterling silver or diamond-encrusted don't count), their materials don't come cheap. Through compression-molding techniques, the Yonex Boroniron and Boronwood clubs combine boron with the same premium-grade carbon graphite cloth used by NASA in the space program. The result is a bona-fide space-age club with a surprisingly traditional shape and design.

A big plus for the Yonex high-tech blend is the "one-piece feel," from the fact that the shaft and the club head are of identical makeup. The idea here is that there is less energy loss when like instead of unlike materials are bonded together. Boron is stiffer than graphite, yet half as heavy as steel, which means that the boron-graphite shaft retains both strength and flexibility, seriously reducing torque, the bane of the everyday hacker. The irons also have a stainless-steel sole plate that serves as a bottom weight to help kick the ball up for higher trajectory.

Another consideration for prospective high-rolling high handicappers is that graphite has great high-repulsion and shock-dampening qualities. This trampoline effect translates into more "give," meaning less wear and effort on the body, as opposed to the harder impact of persimmon club heads and steel shafts. (Graphite has served this function well in the tennis industry, reducing tennis elbow.) To date, most of its use in golf equipment has been limited to shaft construction, because of the difficulty and expense in blending it into the total club.

Minus the boron, the Yonex Carbonex II line is slightly less expensive, but still features densely compacted graphite—each fiber can contain up to five thousand filaments. These clubs have an extremely hard club face, which helps promote exceptional distance. They also have a highly appealing, translucent look about them that is far from traditional. Yonex' high-tech design has a traditional feel, a space-age look and, relatively, an out-of-this-world cost.

## THE POWER POD

For disbelievers, that strange apparatus increasingly sighted on golf tees that resembles a cross between a croquet mallet and an old microphone is actually a golf club—a driver. It is the Orizaba Power Pod, and by the reaction of some golfers you'd think it was equal to the arrival of indoor plumbing.

Developed by Jim Flood (the same man who gave us the Basakwerd putter), the Pod is designed—hold on to your hats—to increase distance and cure a slice. (They don't say anything about the common cold.) Know what? It works.

The Pod has a steel shaft and its head is made out of ground glass mixed with epoxy resins. The hitting area is higher than most drivers (width is the same), which means that you have to use these long, silly-looking tees to get the ball up, but that's a minor inconvenience. The slice-correcting element in the club is its slightly closed club head (turned toward the player). The distance factor—short-hitting players will hit longer—is a result of its pendulous, easy swingability, as well as the symmetry of the club head, which surrounds the ball with proper weight distribution.

The Pod isn't for traditionalists, long hitters or those with pronounced hooks (it can make them worse), but half-swingers and slicers may find added distance and, lo and behold, the middle of the fairway. They just have to be thick-skinned enough to suffer the verbal abuse that may come with using the funny looking club.

The Jack Nicklaus RPM model is one of a growing number of golf clubs designed with the aid of computers. Today, it takes a designer two hours to sketch a blade profile. Two years ago the same work would have taken two weeks to accomplish.

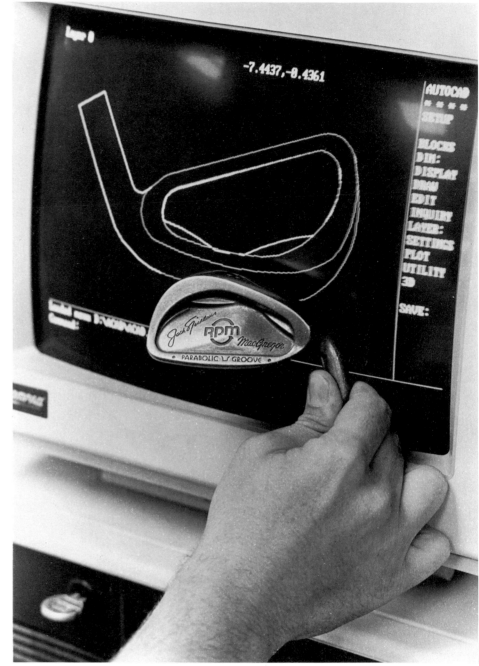

## COMPUTER-AIDED DESIGN (CAD)

Within the space of a few hours, an engineer with some basic computer knowledge can design or refashion a golf club that two decades ago would have taken a year of work. Club design may in a sense still be a traditional craft, but the tools are rapidly changing.

Most "CAD" work is done with an electronic pen that traces an image over the monitor. Then, with a few keyed commands, the club's lie angle, sole width, top-line shape and any number of structural combina-tions can be adjusted. From there an acceptable computer-design blue-print can be fed into a computer-aided manufacturing system (CAM), which will tell machinery how to cut a model to the most precise toler-ances. Presto—a new club.

The major companies can all af-ford the costs of high-tech research and development, since golfers have shown a proclivity for spending that much more to improve their game. Any radical computer changes are not likely, however, because of the rule of golf that states that equip-ment "shall not be substantially dif-ferent from the traditional and cus-tomary form and make."

Still, the computer is a major help on the preliminary level. It took Mac-Gregor's director of research two hours to "sketch" a blade profile for the new RPM line. In 1985, he spent two weeks doing the same job on the Response ZT putter that won the Masters for Jack Nicklaus. Maybe it will take all of a half hour by 1990—and that might still be too slow.

*Right:* The Super Stick is an all-in-one club that takes the place of seventeen clubs. All you need is a coin to adjust loft differential. *Far right:* Slotline's Inertial iron line features heel-to-toe weighting in investment-cast steel. Slotline's most famous club is the Inertial chipper.

## SUPER STICK

The Swiss Army Knife Award for innovative gimmickry goes uncontested to the Highlander Company for creating the Super Stick. For people who don't like to have golf bags or a full complement of bothersome, heavy golf clubs, the Super Stick may be the answer. This seventeen-clubs-in-one package—irons 1 through 9, three different wedges, three putting angles, and a driver—does not, alas, include a ball washer or retriever.

In fairness to the Highlander people, this all-in-one club is meant more for travel convenience than to replace the normal golfing experience. With its adjustable club head, the Super Stick changes loft differential through four sets of interlocking teeth. All you need is a coin to tighten your club selection into position before each shot.

The Super Stick is ingenious enough; however, the club is a bit flimsy in terms of "feel." It's sometimes difficult to realize any difference between the various club angles, and you certainly don't get a solid whack off the "driver." Actually it may be novel, but in functional terms, a Swiss Army knife it ain't.

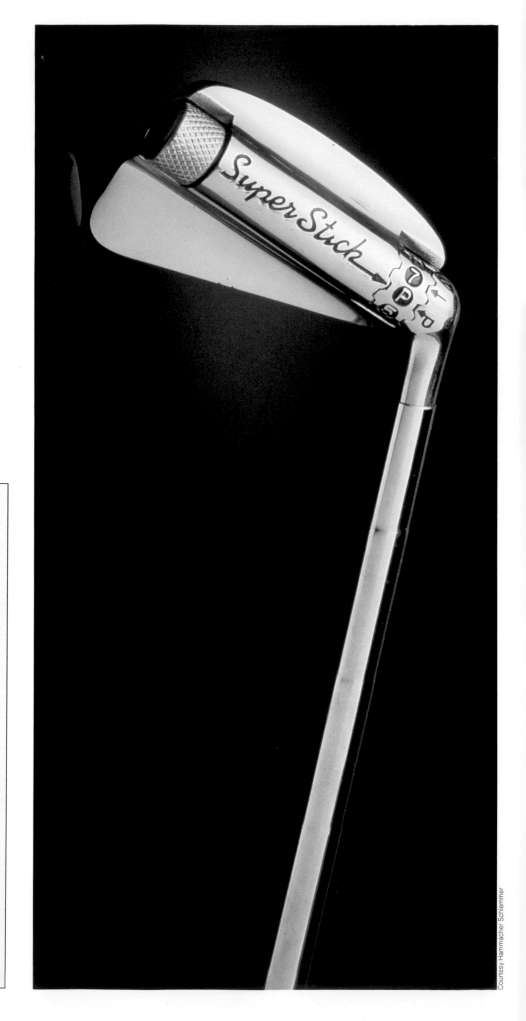

Courtesy Hammacher Schlemmer

# SLOTLINE

*"The good chip allows you to whistle while you walk in the dark alleys of golf."*
—*Tommy Bolt*

The chipper is a sophisticated trouble club that is quite handy for all players unconcerned with the U.S.G.A.'s official fourteen-club-limit rule. It is basically a more refined 7-iron, designed to set up like a putter in fringe grass just off the green.

The Slotline Inertial chipper is made from three metals: aluminum, lead and brass. It is heel-toe weighted, in the manner of putters, and should be swung just like a putter. The club's built-in loft can carry the first few feet of fringe, while the absence of grooves can reduce backspin for straighter, more calculable short approach shots.

Professionals don't carry chippers—they just use a choked-up 7-iron in these situations. But, then again, these fringe shots don't occur that much for the pros; they're usually on the green.

Courtesy The Sharper Image

# TYCOON GRAPHITE IRONS

So maybe you don't want to spend three grand on graphites, but you still like the idea of the club. Maybe Tycoon Graphite irons are the answer. At least you can buy them one at a time for under one hundred dollars each.

The Tycoons are thick, black and compact low-profile irons made of lightweight graphite (shafts also), bolstered with a heavy brass sole plate. The combination makes for an extremely low center of gravity and, theoretically, easy hitting and lofting. Tycoons are made and designed in the style of fairway woods, for those who feel comfortable hitting with that club.

# TRUE TEMPER

If you own a set of golf clubs, the odds are good that you're using one brand or another of True Temper shafts. In 1924, the U.S.G.A., aware that the wooden shaft was doomed by a depletion of hickory, reluctantly okayed the use of steel shafts. Ever since then, True Temper has dominated the field. Originally the American Fork & Hoe Manufacturing Co., True Temper makes sixty-five percent of the shafts produced today, including a representation of over ninety percent at the 1987 U.S. Open.

The hallmark of True Temper shaft design is the step-tapering pattern that controls the different wall diameters and thicknesses from tip (bottom) to butt (top). The shafts are made from high-alloy steel with many weights and flexes available. The extra stiff "Dynamic" model is the one traditionally used by professionals, since its high flex produces optimum trajectory for backspin hitters. On the other end, the "ExtraLite" combines a featherweight quality with the new "TTX" steel, the strongest alloy they use. In between are five different brands for every level of golfer.

## SAND WEDGE

*"The object of a bunker or trap is not only to punish a physical mistake—to punish a lack of control—but also to punish pride and egotism."*
—*Charles Blair Macdonald, golf-course architect.*

The great Gene Sarazen, along with the best of his contemporaries, was repeatedly punished for the arrogance of trying to carry long shots over sand traps. The problem back then was what to do when an errant strike found the beach. Bobby Jones and Walter Hagen were notoriously bad sand players—the explosion shot was virtually unheard of and couldn't be effected anyway, for lack of a proper club. At some point during the 1931 season, a fed-up Sarazen went down to his basement and invented the sand wedge. He took a standard niblick (9-iron) and added a deep flange to the back. This created the possibility of bouncing through the sand to accurately "blast" a ball from a bunker to the pin. It wasn't long before all top players took advantage. Today, the sand wedge is, next to the putter, the professional's single most indispensable club; its use by skilled players has reduced sand traps to a minor nuisance—skilled players, that is.

*Left:* True Temper—the standard shaft of the golf club industry. *Below and right:* The art of the "explosion" shot from out of the sand. The shot would have never evolved without the sand wedge.

While retaining the same basic shapes, modern club design has nevertheless changed quite a bit in the past twenty years. Here are examples of modern club design. The iron is investment-cast and cavity-backed and the woods are offset with radiused soles.

## CLUB TALK PRIMER

Today's golf club design can be divided into two categories: traditional and game-improvement. The simpler, traditional irons feature forged musclebacked club heads, long hosels and conventional setback. The ever-changing game-improvement irons usually feature investment-cast, perimeter-weighted (sometimes hollow), cavity-backed club heads, with varying degrees of offset. Traditional woods are pear-shaped and made of persimmon or laminated woods, while the latest "woods" can be made of anything from graphite to ground glass and can include features that vary from radiused soles to backweight inserts. Got that? If it all sounds like Chinese algebra, here's a primer that might help you translate your golf professional's sales pitch into English.

**OFFSET** occurs when the leading edge (bottom) of the iron's (or, sometimes, wood's) club face is set back from the hosel (the piece that connects the head to the shaft). This positions a player's hands slightly in front of the ball and encourages a square club face at impact, which will help promote accuracy and control wildness.

**INVESTMENT-CASTING** is a process for making iron club heads by pouring molten metal into a ceramic shell that has been molded to specifications. It is very accurate for insuring that a "matched set" is precisely just that—that the loft differential from club to club is proportionally correct. It also redistributes the club-head weight.

**PERIMETER-WEIGHTING** is an innovation that allows the weight to be spread out around the club head and removed from directly behind the hitting area. This reduces the degree of twist on mishits and enlarges the "sweet spot" area.

**FORGED** irons are made by heating a metal bar, then placing it between the two halves of a metal die until the club head gradually takes shape. Imperfections are then ground and polished out.

**MUSCLEBACK** is the buildup of mass where the blade bulges on the back of a forged-iron club head.

**LOW-PROFILE** irons have shortened club faces, the intention being to lower the center of gravity, making it easier to hit the ball in the air.

**CAVITY-BACKED** irons have large club heads with a recessed area on the back where the weight has been removed and redistributed around the club head's extremities, mainly in the wider sole.

A **RADIUSED SOLE** is the curved underside of many modern clubs; this allows average players a more proper address from a variety of lies.

# PUTTERS

*"Confidence builds with successive putts. The putter, then, is a club designed to hit the ball partway to the hole."*
                    —Rex Lardner, Out of the Bunker and Into the Trees, 1960.

For the centuries that golf was played in its cruder forms, there were no putters, as there were no putting greens, only holes in the ground. Once putting areas became better defined, in the 1800s, a sort of abbreviated wood (spoons) became fashionable for the short game. The modern-day putter owes its provenance both to the advances of metal irons in the late nineteenth century and to the need for a specialized club to stroke the ball toward the hole on the groomed, carpetlike surfaces of the new putting greens.

While there are thousands of different putters available on the market today, all but a few are variations on (or combinations of) two basic themes: the gooseneck blade and the mallet head. The former first appeared in 1896, as designed by Scotsman Willie Park, and was the prototype for the famous "Calamity Jane," used by Bobby Jones in the twenties: The latter was first seen at the British Amateur in 1904 in the hands of the American winner, Walter Travis, after which it was banned for forty-seven years.

The following is a selection of some of the most celebrated and popular over the years, as well as some of the most innovative, putters available today.

As surfaces of the "modern" greens improved, so evolved the modern putter. *Below left:* A left-handed "generic" version of Arnold Palmer's old putter. *Below:* The Hogan Apex putter, like many of today's putters, draws on not-so-subtle influences from the Ping line.

Ping's latest Pal
models are varia-
tions on Solheim's
original Anser.

## ANSER (Ping)

Karsten Solheim, future patriarch of the Ping dynasty, was only trying to "find an answer" to all the other putters, when, around 1960, he designed an ungainly club based on a revolutionary concept. By placing almost all of the club's weight in its heel and its toe, he found he could reduce twisting on mishits by more than fifty percent. He liked the name "answer," but thought it looked too long written on the back of the club, so he dropped the "w." Eventually, Solheim would name all of his clubs after the distinctive atonal "ping" sound of his putter.

Of equal importance to the performance of a Ping putter is the alignment of its shaft to its scooped-out head, as connected by a goose-necked elbow joint. This creates the right amount of vibration for what Solheim calls the proper "moment of inertia" in the face.

If that last line sounds like some mystical sales pitch, consider the fact that over half the field of every professional tournament uses a Ping putter—there are over eighty models based around similar designs—and many of the remaining players use an imitation made by a competitor. Despite the strange look, Ping putters are a perfect example of blending mallet head and blade styles.

One of the conveniences of Ping putters is the ball-scooping configuration of the back of the putter head, which saves golfers from bending over on greens—a feature totally eschewed by professionals and scoffed at by traditionalists. It seems real men don't go for golf gadgetry. Still, the Anser will go down as the putter of the eighties, maybe even longer, unless another more revolutionary club surfaces.

Courtesy Karsten Manufacturing Corp./Ping Golf Clubs

*Courtesy Karsten Manufacturing Corp./Ping Golf Clubs*

*Courtesy Spalding Sports Worldwide*

# DAVE PELZ

*"Different? The key word is playable."* —Dave Pelz, physicist and golf-club designer.

When is a putter not a putter—legally, that is—according to the United States Golf Association? With regards to the Pelz putter—called the "club that gave birth to triplets"—the U.S.G.A. says the company's big model is legal, but the small one isn't.

The three balls in a row on the back of the Pelz putter are intended to optically ease the task of putting alignment. The theory is that the line of four balls (including the one in play) will visually aid stroking the ball more directly to the hole.

The U.S.G.A.'s problem is with Pelz' blade, which doesn't conform to rule 41d: "The length of the club head, from heel to toe, shall be greater than the breadth, from front to back." So Pelz now has two models available: one with the small blade in front of the balls (illegal) and one with the large blade (legal), which has been used to varying degrees of success by the pros. One observation is undeniable—the club was never designed to be aesthetically appealing.

# CASH-IN

If you've ever rented or borrowed old golf clubs, chances are you've probably used the Cash-in putter that usually winds up with the set. You know, that plain thing, with the oblong chrome club head that looks just like a putter ought to look (or at least the way they used to ought to look). It has a line notched across the top, which may or may not be of help in hitting the ball dead center. The typical nicks and scars found on opposite ends of the club face would seem to indicate that this line has gone ignored for most of the club's life.

The Cash-in took its name from a little-known "Mr. Cash," who sold it to Spalding in 1929. Fifty years and a few million putters later, Spalding makes a sleeker, updated facsimile called the TPM 11. This more refined putter is black with white cross hairs on the club face and has a cambered sole and a rounded toe, as opposed to its flat-bottomed, square-toed predecessor. It also works better.

*Left:* The Ping Zing 2, resembling a mini-banana boat, is the most extreme of Karsten Solheim's new putters. *Above:* Spalding's reasonable facsimile of the Cash-in— probably the simplest no-frills putter design ever.

*Below:* The Bullseye, virtually intact since 1946, when its owner hawked it from stop to stop on the pro tour.
*Right:* The oversized Response line of putters became immediately successful after Nicklaus won the Masters in 1986 with the same huge putter.

## BULLSEYE (Titleist)

The Bullseye putter, invented in 1946 by a Michigan pro named John Reuter, Jr., is a more streamlined version of the old Cash-in. The contours of the putter head faintly resemble a genie's lamp, and its appearance may well have been magical at the time. For fifteen years, Reuter sold the Bullseye at stops on the pro tour, until the club was bought out by Titleist in 1962.

Except for the recent addition of offset and a distinctly rounded sole, the thin, brass-bladed Bullseye has remained virtually intact since 1946. With its concentrated and balanced, pendulous feel, the club introduced a more weighty, calibrated quality to putter design. Today it can be bought in just about every pro shop in the world.

## 8802 (Wilson)

Throughout his career, Arnold Palmer has had a problem deciding on putters. In 1963, he designed himself a flanged, forged-blade model to be made by Wilson. Its use by the great one hardly escaped his multitude of fans, and the club's immediate success was all but guaranteed. Palmer did leave Wilson soon after to start his own company, but the club survived and has been called by its stock number ever since. Palmer still uses it sometimes, or at least a prototype of it—that is, when he's not using one of two dozen other putters.

# RESPONSE ZT (MacGregor)

Most golfers who watched Jack Nicklaus's amazing come-from-behind victory in the 1986 Masters found it hard to ignore that monstrous oversize putter that seemed to roll and steer those long putts into the cup, hole after hole. Naturally, sales of the Response ZT soared the following week.

When Nicklaus first tried the club on his home practice green he liked neither the looks nor the feel of it. (MacGregor never designed the club for him in the first place.) He quickly got over his prejudice when, after a few practice strokes, he found he couldn't miss a putt. The ZT's (zero twist) humongous club face is designed to make it easier to line up the ball (yes, even Nicklaus has these problems) and is also machined to a thousandth of an inch of perfect flatness for accurate "response."

Leave the final word on the club to MacGregor president George Nichols, who sums up its basic premise with irrefutable logic: "What's easier to aim, a pistol or a rifle?"

## THE SCHENECTADY PUTTER

One of the first pieces of golf equipment ever to become widely known and sought out was the "Schenectady," a putter named after its obscure designer's home town. In 1904, Walter Travis became the first American ever to win the British Amateur, thanks largely to his spectacular play on the greens with the new mallet-headed putter. The cigar-smoking putting wizard rapidly popularized the club, although it was as much Travis's soft touch as anything else that was responsible for his success on the greens.

Also, for the first time a putter's shaft was attached at the center of the head. This was enough for the club to be barred by the British in 1909—along with any other croquet-style putters—for not conforming to traditional design. The ban on center-shafted putters lasted more than fifty years, during which time the Schenectady had a brief run of popularity in the United States, where it was still legal. But by the time the ban was lifted the club's usage was practically obsolete.

# BASAKWERD (Orizaba)

Desperate golfers, of whom there are many, will try anything to cure their putting ills. Such was the case of inventor Jim Flood when, while practicing in 1982, he turned his putter around, facing towards his feet. Eureka!

Inspired, Flood developed the Basakwerd, the club so named for its look, which, with shaft meeting blade on the far (opposite) side of the stick, is more like a garden hoe than a putter. The main reason for the bizarre club's efficiency is its pendulum-like "swingability," which helps putts hold their line and makes "pushing" (stroking to the right) all but impossible.

If the Basakwerd has a problem, it lies in its appearance, which some may find too difficult and awkward to become mentally comfortable with. The club is still used by a few top pros (mostly on the Seniors tour), though it never really took off. Still and all, it's a must for many of golfdom's seekers and searchers.

# SLIM JIM (Matzie)

*"From five feet to the hole, you're in the throw up zone."*—Dave Hill, Teed Off, 1977.

The "yips," a psychological imbalance that can quadruple the length of an eighteen-inch putt, pays an occasional visit to all golfers at one time or another. The best one can hope for is that this anguished state does not become a permanent condition—although for many it inevitably does. Charlie Owens, a senior pro with just such a bad case, set out to cure himself by designing a correctional putter for the nerve-racked. By succeeding, he may have kept a few hackers out of the nuthouse.

The Slim Jim, Owens' contribution to mental health on the links, is over four feet tall, yet weighs only one and a half pounds. The mallet-headed club, illegal on the regular tour, has been eagerly embraced by over thirty percent of senior professionals, Sam Snead among them.

The principle of the Slim Jim is that it allows you to stand upright and see the entire line of short putts more accurately. The stroke is a sidesaddle croquet swipe, with the left hand directing the club at the top and the right hand providing the sweeping motion down below. By eliminating the need to bend over, the club also helps avoid lower-back strain, an ailment that, not coincidentally, often travels with the yips. With the Slim Jim, Owens won over $200,000 in prize money in 1986, as well as a legion of appreciative fans.

# ZEBRA (Ram)

Designed in the mid-seventies, the Zebra, from Ram Golf, is the classic mallet-headed putter, as well as an awesome-looking instrument. (Can you maybe drive with this thing?) The club draws its name from the stripes on its head, which are intended to aid alignment. The current model has an "access weighting" chamber system that allows you to make adjustments by adding or removing weights, depending on the speed or roll of different greens. This may or may not be necessary to your game, and it may not endear you to your playing partners.

Putting is perhaps the most nerve-racking aspect of golf. Billy Casper is generally regarded as the greatest putter of all time.

*BALLS*

*"Laddie, throw me that ball. I thought so. The bugger isn't round."*
—Arthur Lees, British pro, after missing a thirty foot putt.

If golf is relatively affordable today—an arguable point to begin with—it was prohibitively expensive before 1848. Until then, flailing away at the little ball was exclusively the province of the very rich. That we can pin down such a clear-cut transitional passage lies solely with the revolutionary and well-documented arrival of the gutta-percha ball.

For centuries, golf was played with the feathery ball, made of three pieces of bull's hide sewn together, into which boiled-down goose feathers were packed through a small hole. A skilled Scottish ballmaker could produce only four "featheries" a day, each costing four times the price of a golf club.

The earliest guttas-perchas, hand-fashioned from the Malaysian gum extract of the same name, cost roughly one-third the price of a club (today's golf balls are about one-twentieth) and did not have to be crafted by artisans. The first "guttas" had smooth exteriors, until it was quickly realized that as a ball accumulated the usual nicks and cuts it flew better. The ensuing process of hand-hammering a ball's exterior—a skilled worker could pound three hundred little dents into a ball inside two minutes—gave way to machine molding by the 1870s.

In 1902, the modern three-piece golf ball was born composed of a rubber core around which hundreds of yards of thin rubber thread were wound, and an outer covering of gutta-percha (later balata or Surlyn). BF Goodrich developed and sold the "Haskell" ball (named after its inventor), also derogatorily called the "Bounding Billie," for its ability to roll and hop down the fairway after a mishit shot. Aside from the aerodynamically important addition of inverted dimples (1910-20), and some changes in the toughness and elasticity of rubber, we're basically playing the same type of ball today.

New balls may appear on the golf marketplace every other day, but almost all are constructed in one of two fashions: two-piece, with a hard rubber core and plastic cover; or three piece, with a liquid or rubber core, rubber windings and either a soft balata cover or a hard cover.

Typical marketing hypes would have you believe that every ball travels farther, lasts longer and sails straighter than the next. Believe this: every ball is only as good as the golfer who strikes it. Still, there are subtleties to the little things, even if most golfers would be hard pressed to tell balls apart on blind tests. The mere idea that a golf ball might perform predictably may give a golfer some sense of security (however short-lived), and that counts for a lot.

## THE COLLECTOR

"I just started picking the stupid things up," Ted Myers of Marietta, Georgia, likes to say about his penchant for collecting golf balls. It all started in 1983, when after heart surgery the doctors told Myers, who lives on a golf course, that he had to take walks. Telling a golfer to walk without golfing is like having a gambler watch horse races without betting. So Myers put his time to good use by bending over on occasion; he now has amassed over fifteen thousand balls, with no two alike, ranging from balls with advertising logos to balls from country clubs to balls from little-known pros from the past. "It's gotten completely out of hand," he tells everybody.

Of course, there's a limit to how many different kinds of balls you can find on one course, so Myers has become a true collector, attending auctions and trading duplicates with other collectors. What constitutes value for Myers in a contemporary golf ball? "Any ball that has something printed on it that I don't have."

Myers has most of the balls resting on one-by-two-inch wooden racks scattered around his house. Ball companies are quick to send him complimentary dozens of their latest models so they can be included in his displays. He has allocated room for another three or four thousand, and he sees no end to his collecting. These days, Myers has taken up golf again, about twice a week, and it shouldn't surprise anyone that he can't remember the last time he bought a golf ball.

Traditional golf ball displays are very popular among contemporary collectors. Ted Myers, possessor of one of the world's largest collections, has over fifteen thousand balls, with no two alike.

*Below:* Spalding, the largest manufacturer of golf balls, sports a new line practically every other year. *Opposite page:* Maxfli golf balls are known for their unique dimple configurations. Their latest is a dodecahedron (DDH), made up of twelve pentagons.

## SPALDING

The first company to manufacture golf balls in the United States, Spalding, was also the first to make the dimpled ball, after a 1905 patent by an English golfer of note, William Taylor. The value of these dimples—which became the industry standard by 1930—cannot be overestimated. They help the ball get airborne and make it go farther. The game is difficult enough today—let's not even think about the old balls. Please!

In 1968, Spalding developed the Top-Flite, the first two-piece ball, made of a hard, uniform rubber core, encased in a new super-tough plastic called Surlyn. This ball—as made by Spalding and other firms—has become the distance ball, significantly longer both in carry and roll. With the durable Surlyn shell, the ball has proven itself practically immune to cutting and rarely ever loses its shape or compression.

The world's best-selling golf ball is the two-piece Spalding Top-Flite "XL," designed to give higher trajectory and lift for those who tend to hit on a lower than average plane off the tees. A close relative to the XL is the Top-Flite "Plus," which offers over one hundred added dimples (492 total), translating into extra carry and even higher shots that are more likely to hold the greens.

The most recent Spalding addition is the Top-Flite "II" for those who truly want to cream the ball. Designed for long hitters, this ball has a pattern of two different-sized dimples, resulting in a lower trajectory and improved flight. The ball is ideal for boring through a head wind.

Realistically, the only drawback to Top-Flites and other two-piece balls needs only apply to low-handicap players—that is, the minimal amount of backspin generated, making it more difficult to maneuver on approach shots. Since the average golfer can't properly apply underspin or backspin anyway, it should be no loss. In the same vein, professionals can all consistently hit the bleep out of the ball anyway, so why should they sacrifice control for a fraction of added distance?

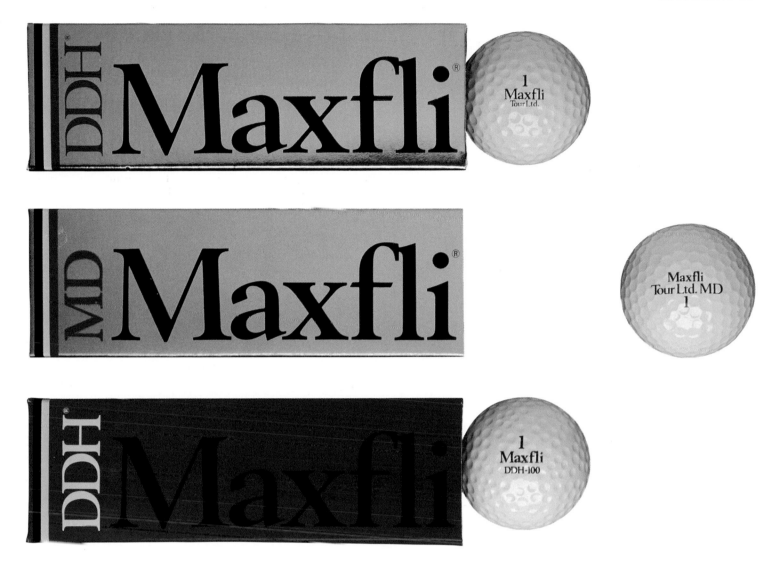

# DUNLOP

With the invention of an odd-looking, moon-cratered golf ball that lays claim to higher mathematics (and better mileage), the Dunlop Maxfli line may have a chance to gain some ground on the market-dominating Top-Flites and Titleists. It's all in the dimples, say the Dunlop scientists, creators of the two-piece Maxfli "DDH."

The ball's design was literally born on the back of cocktail napkins in an English pub, where a group of Dunlop researchers and mathematicians had gathered for some after-hours libation. The subject of discussion was ultimate golf-ball symmetry, and how to attain a surface pattern of such physical uniformity and aerodynamic consistency as to insure maximum flight stability (i.e. make the ball go straight). Out of those scribblings—and five years of research and testing—came the dodecahedron (DDH) dimple pattern, composed of twelve pentagons.

The dodecahedron configuration represents what Dunlop calls "geometric integrity," with each pentagon containing thirty dimples of four different sizes. The larger, shallow dimples scoop the wind for increased velocity, while the smaller, deeper dimples give more controlled flight. The result is a low-flying bullet that will cut through a gale and roll a country mile.

The perfect golf ball? Well, the DDH hasn't turned the industry upside down, although Dunlop does have an exclusive patent that precludes any copies. Fuzzy Zoeller, Hal Sutton and a handful of other well-known professionals have used the ball successfully, which, again, may not be relevant to the average golfer. With a healthy poke, he or she will surely benefit from the low arc and added roll. But with that goofy look, it's a big surprise that the DDH acts like a golf ball at all. It does; it may even be the longest ball.

## BALL RULES

The U.S.G.A., in concert with the Royal and Ancient Golf Club of St. Andrews, ultimately decides what constitutes a legitimate golf ball. Over three hundred makes have received U.S.G.A. approval, based on an exacting set of standards. Without the rules, an already confusing situation (what type ball to play?) would be chaotic.

For starters, a ball must weigh no more than 1.62 ounces and must measure at least 1.68 inches in circumference. These standards are set in order to keep balls from being too small or too heavy, either of which can increase distance.

Pressed by industry advances, the U.S.G.A. in 1976 added the Overall Distance Standard—that a ball shall not travel over 296.8 yards when struck by Iron Byron, the mechanical golfer that repeatedly reproduces a perfect golfer's swing. (The machine is named after golf great Byron Nelson, who also had a repeatedly perfect swing.) New balls, designed for maximum distance, constantly threaten the limit while trying to gain every conceivable advantage.

Also laboratory-tested, before a golf ball receives U.S.G.A. approval, is something called "initial velocity performance," by which flight speed shall not be allowed to exceed 250 feet per second.

Finally, a ball must pass the symmetry standard, by flying the same height and distance and remaining airborne the same length of time, no matter how it is placed on the tee. This is because minute changes in a ball's contours can, in combination with an educated golf swing and the right placement on a tee, unfairly aid a player in directing the flight path.

# NITELITE

The scene is a familiar one to the hard-core golfer: Dusk is setting in at about the fifteenth hole, but the round must be finished at all costs. By the seventeenth, he can barely see the ball at his feet, much less hit it and then find it. At the eighteenth tee, it's pitch dark, he can hardly make out his partner; the round is, for all intents and purposes, over, ruined by a half-dozen lost balls on the last hole.

This common scenario needs no longer be played out, thanks to a brilliant idea called the "Nitelite." Invented by Pinprick Enterprises in 1986, the Nitelite is a glow-in-the-dark golf ball that can be seen up to one hundred yards in the dead of night. Its bright-green glow is emitted by a lightstick that is inserted into a regulation-sized, translucent golf ball. The luminescence lasts up to eight hours, and the ball has the same feel and flight as a regulation ball, except for a ten percent loss in distance. The U.S.G.A. won't legalize it, on the ground that it gives a player an unfair advantage over his opponent. But people who play in the dark can't be too fussy about rules.

# CAYMAN

Shame on Jack Nicklaus anyway. While the rest of the golf world continues its search for the longest ball, he goes and designs one that is geared to cut distance in half. Some nerve for a guy who can hit the ball much farther than most mortals.

The "Cayman" is the MacGregor-Nicklaus contribution toward space-efficient shorter courses of the future. The ball is named after just such a course in the Caribbean that looks like it could fit in a parking lot. The Cayman weighs sixty percent less than an ordinary ball and has convex, inverted dimples, for a short, accurate trajectory.

The principle idea is to make golf more economical. With the short ball, the game could conceivably be played on one-quarter of the land of a regular course, with one-third the clubs, in half the time. Taking a full swing with a driver, Nicklaus hits the Cayman about 135 yards. He says he's not trying to "revolutionize anything," but is only concerned with golf space in the future. "If you use a golf ball that goes only half as far," reasons Nicklaus, "you need only one-fourth the land, because your dimensions are reduced in both directions."

Invented by Pinprick Enterprises in 1986, the regulation-sized, translucent Nitelite uses a lightstick that makes it glow in the dark. Play through dusk... and then some.

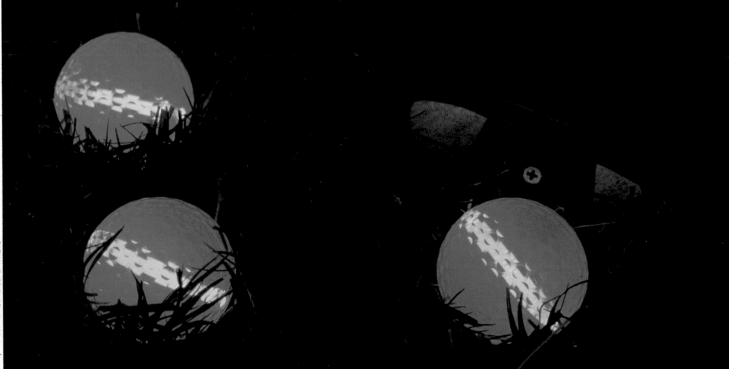
Courtesy The Golf Works/©Randall D. Williams

The Floater does just that; it floats. Available in most pro shops, this ball has found increasing use at a number of over-water driving ranges.

## GOOF BALLS

For all the pranksters who like to lighten up a round of golf, there's never an end in sight to the innovative gimmickry that follows the game's industry. Most of the following items are purely meant for un-guaranteed fun. Know your partner and proceed with caution.

The "Floater," found in most pro shops, is just that, a floating golf ball. It was designed to help golfers overcome the fear of hitting over water—although for long hazards, they'll need a bathing suit to go retrieve it. It looks like a regular ball, has a rubber composition, and is, naturally, lighter than normal, resulting in 10% less distance. Recently, the floater has found a home at an increasing number of driving ranges that are over water.

The "Exploder" and the "Goofy Ball" are for practical jokers and should definitely be kept away from the serious set. The Exploder is made of talcum powder and will detonate harmlessly when struck by a club. The problem is switching your opponent's ball when he's not looking, then getting him to accept this highly suspect, unmarked sphere. Intended for a putting-green switch, the Goofy Ball has its weight all on one side and is guaranteed not to go into the hole.

The "Renegade" is an illegal ball and proud of it. For those who make up their own rules, the Renegade is slightly smaller and heavier than U.S.G.A. guidelines allow. The ball, in fact, has never been submitted for approval and lays claims to an extra twenty yards off the tee. The price for the extra distance may be the gradual disappearance of playing partners, once they realize what's up.

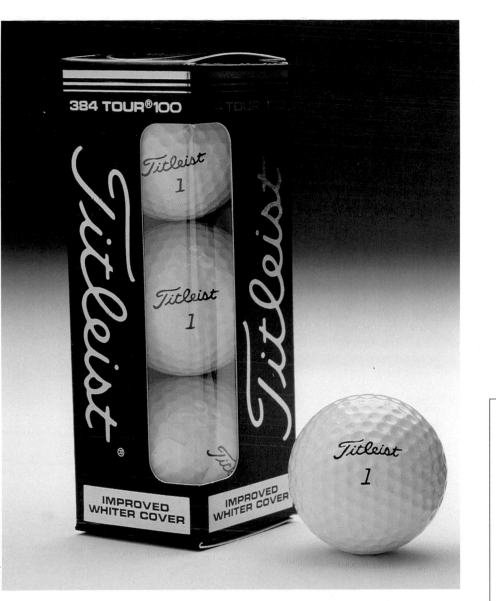

Courtesy Titleist Golf Division

## TITLEIST

Regardless of what other ball makers may claim, the Titleist ball is the overwhelming choice of professionals. In 1987, over seventy percent of all tournament golfers played Titleists—at the U.S. Open, the figure was even higher: ninety percent. In fact, if a pro does play and push any other brand of ball, you can bet it's only because he's paid plenty to do so. Even then, he still may slip in a Titleist for a round or two, although he must be careful—losing an endorsement can be the price of getting caught.

The primary reason for Titleist's success among the best of players has to do with the "feel" or "touch" associated with the ball, particularly the "384 Tour" model. The soft balata covering, along with the three-piece construction (rubber windings, pre-frozen liquid core) and icosahedral dimple pattern, combine for the most "workable" golf ball, one that sacrifices little or no distance. By workable, we're talking about a quality that allows great spin to be imparted on the ball, for better lift, control and bite—all staples of the pro game.

By X-raying golf balls, Titleist founder Phil Young discovered in 1932 that most cores were severely distorted and off center, resulting in erratic performance. Decades of research and testing corrected the problem, and today Titleist still x-rays their balls.

Naturally, many ordinary hackers like to play Titleists because of their great reputation among the professionals. But one deterrent for the lesser skilled should be the soft outer cover (except for the "384 DT" model)—it tends to cut rather easily when topped, shanked or generally not hit well.

It was not unusual for some British golfers to deliver personal poems about life on the links to various golf periodicals. The following ode was written by J. H. Hayes and appeared in *Golf Illustrated* around the turn of the century.

*TO A GOLF BALL*
Long ago when I first bought you,
  You were white and fairly round,
And a little gem I thought you,
  Teed upon the teeing ground.

But, alas! The months have vanished,
  And, if I must speak the truth,
They have altogether banished
  The resemblance to your youth.

For I've "pulled" you and I've "sliced" you,
  And you've lain in banks of gorse,
And I've temptingly enticed you
  From the cart-ruts on the course.

So, though quite devoid of beauty,
  I would claim you as a friend
Who has nobly done his duty
  From beginning to the end.

And receive my thinks unsparing,
  That you've heard with dumb assent,
The perhaps too-frequent swearing
  Which I've used though never meant.

## DIMPLES

Without dimples, the golf ball wouldn't go very far (actually, about half as far as with dimples, according to U.S.G.A. testing). With the natural spin from a golf shot, dimples operate like gears that pull the ball skyward, gripping and easing the air around to the back of the ball, thus reducing the resistance. Lift is a result of the ball pressing against the decreased drag. Eventually, as the spin and speed slow, gravity will win out, and the ball will fall.

For forty years, the most common pattern was the straight-line, or "octahedral," pattern, which featured four circular rows across the top and four across the bottom, with little triangles of dimples filling out the empty spaces. There are a few balls still made this way—probably for diehard purists—but today's technology has left octahedrals behind.

In 1974, Titleist came out with the "icosahedral" pattern that currently accounts for over ninety percent of all ball design. Here, the surface is divided into twenty equal triangular dimple groups. The idea is that as the ball spins and rotates, it offers an identical pattern to the air it contacts with, drastically reducing resistance. The result is a higher trajectory with more carry, though less roll. This is beneficial in that it drops the ball off at a sharper angle at its apex, for better control.

The most radical dimple grouping is Dunlop's "dodecahedral" setup, which, to the naked eye, looks random, but is actually made up of twelve pentagons. Wilson wraps triangles around pentagons for something called IMPL (icosahedral multiple parting line).

Much simpler to grasp than all of the above is simple total dimple count, which for decades stood at around 324 per ball. No longer. Titleist's 384 sets the industry standard, with Nicklaus-MacGregor and Ben Hogan balls coming in slightly higher at 392, and Wilson's Ultra at 432. Top-Flite Plus is currently the most cavity-filled, with 492, but a Japanese company will soon be coming out with a 600-plus model—all in search of the perfect golf ball.

## COLORED BALLS

The reason for the creation of the orange ball by Wilson, in 1982, was that it would be harder to lose. For certain, it's easier to find. Just ask any golfer who's spent the better part of a round searching for traditionally white lost balls, only to wind up with a bagful of "orange-aids." Also called "pumpkins," these orange balls were all the rage when they first came out, prompting other ballmakers to follow suit with their own versions. Today, the choice has expanded to turquoise, chartreuse, violet, pink—even a dizzying two-tone model. The colors, once painted on, are now blended into the outer plastic to eliminate chipping. Colored balls are, however, virtually unused by professionals and have bottomed out at twenty percent of the market from a onetime high of fifty percent.

# BAGS

Typical century-old photos or drawings of golf matches usually portray the day's crusty caddies with an assortment of clubs carried loose under the arms or slung over the shoulder by means of a simple strap. The first golf bags didn't arrive until the late 1890s, prompted by the need for a more efficient means of hauling one's own sticks when without the privilege of a live caddy. These early bags, called "club carriers," were functional and lightweight (often canvas), with one small ball pouch on the side. Sometimes a steel stake or frame on the back was added for standing the bag upright.

For the mammoth modern golf bag—meant to be lugged only by stout-hearted caddies or hauled with the aid of golf carts or golf cars—we can thank one L. E. Pilkington, who in 1914 designed side compartments for boots, sweaters, etc. and a divider at the mouth to separate woods and irons. In the years leading up to the fourteen-club-limit rule (1938), bag size grew in direct proportion to the amount of clubs carried—often as many as twenty-five to thirty. Today's big bags, as seen on the pro tour, can hold enough golf clubs for a foursome, several wardrobe changes and a spare kitchen sink. For traveling professionals, the added space can actually be useful for transporting duplicate clubs, rainwear and the assorted staples needed for life on the tour. For the average player? He just likes to look like a pro.

©Gerald L. French /FPG International

*Left:* A typical modern bag. *Below:* Many manufacturers don't let you off with a mere purchase: your new bag serves as a billboard for their products. *Opposite page:* Club dividers help keep the most compulsive golfers' clubs organized.

©Patrick Ward/Wheeler Pictures

# MILLER

Unlike many golf manufacturers who put out everything you need to play the game (clubs, balls, bag, gloves, etc.), Ron Miller Associates makes only golf bags—nine hundred a day. They make every kind: big fat tour models (10½ inches in diameter at the top); pink, banana or sky-blue ladies types; increasingly popular lightweight nylon bags; and even little scaled-down "Bottle Caddy" specials for stashing booze.

The large vinyl "Tour" models look like they could survive a drop down a side of the Grand Canyon, even if they are only going to be asked to spend their days reclining on the back of a golf car. Some of the features are: three-ring steel construction, polyethylene liners, non-jamming zippers (a big plus), full-length dividers and dual drag plates on the bottom (sounds like a car extra). Most of this is all fine, but are the double-tiered ball pouches really necessary? Couldn't all the balls be stored in one pocket?

Junior vice-president Bill Miller equates a golfer's need for larger bags with a common obsession: "just like wanting a larger automobile." But Miller will also stress that the more functional nylon bags have grown to sixty-five percent of his company's business, making the same headway as economy cars. (This may have something to do with walking and the fitness craze of the eighties.) One thing's for certain: You do not walk a round of golf with a Miller "Tour" or "Deluxe" model around your shoulders—not unless you're a pro caddy who is getting well paid for it.

# PING (Karsten Manufacturing)

You play golf; you walk the course; you carry your own bag. You don't own a pull-cart; you don't rent electric carts. You're a distinct minority and probably healthier for it.

Karsten has an attractive, functional bag designed especially for walkers. Leave it to the company that designs the most popular and functional of golf clubs (Ping) to come up with the most functional of lightweight bags. In this case, they've actually made them attractive as well.

The Ping "Lite Carry" bag is an economic energy-saver made of water-repellent nylon. It has an eight-inch diameter, will hold a full set of clubs, and weights only thirty-seven ounces. A wood stay provides sturdiness and keeps the bag from collapsing when standing or leaning, a common failure of most lightweight models. The two side pockets (one large enough for clothing) are perfectly adequate for walkers—most of whom tend to travel light anyway, which is what this bag is all about. It comes in ten tasteful colors—no mauve, burgundy, lavender or chartreuse.

# PULL-CARTS

In 1897, E. E. B. Boehmer took out a patent for the golf "trolley," forerunner of today's ubiquitous pull-carts. In the patent, Boehmer explained the purpose: "...whereby the dumb caddies may be pulled or pushed over the ground on wheels instead of carried."

The first prototype, circa 1900, was the "Rover" Golf Caddie, somewhat fraudulently advertised at the time "for ease and comfort." Its problems were twofold: small, hard wheels that didn't roll well—especially over hilly links layouts—and the absence of a handle for pulling. At any rate, functional pull-carts didn't appear until the late 1940s; during the following twenty years their use became widespread.

*Above:* The three-wheeled Kanga-roo "motor-caddie" is a poor man's caddie that won't talk back. *Right:* Goodbye back strain. The pull-cart is one of the greatest, if not *the* greatest, of all golf's many innovations.

# BROWNING

Browning's Bag Boy line of pull-carts dates back to 1946, when Bruce Williamson designed a little-known, untried product out of two lawn-mower wheels and a spring-suspension chassis. Following this concept, the manufacture of basic carts began, using sand castings and aluminum tubing, with all parts bolted together.

Today, Bag Boy is the largest cart manufacturer in the game. If the brand name is not universally synonymous with the product, it's probably only because pull-carts are something most golfers take for granted, especially rentals. You simply will not hear someone ask a pro what make of carts he has for rent—probably Bag Boy "Rentals" anyway.

The most popular cart in the game is the Bag Boy "Spartan" model, which sports a bag-retention system–something ordinary rental carts sorely lack, as evidenced by the spill-on-the-hill scene, which can unexpectedly embarrass all but the most experienced cart handlers. All Bag Boy carts come with a five-year warranty.

Naturally, Bag Boy has a luxury model, the "Master," replete with 12½-inch white tires, gold-trimmed bag brackets, and, yes, hubcaps. A "spectator seat" that rides alongside the bag is optional. The attached white vinyl stool can come in handy on hot midsummer days, which should offset some of the jibes that are sure to come, free of charge.

# KANGAROO

From the "why-hadn't-they-thought-of-it-sooner?" department comes the "Kangaroo" electronic golf-bag carrier, or "motorcaddie," from Hillcrest. (Actually, the Kangaroo dates back to 1970; it's just never taken golfdom by storm.) The motorcaddie is basically a motorized golf cart that travels ahead of the golfer. Battery-powered and with a sealed-in transmission, it has a speed control that allows your clubs to match your walking pace. The idea is that you may want to walk without the "exertion" of pulling or pushing your clubs, especially on hilly terrain.

The design of the Kangaroo is hardly streamlined; the visible battery and motor have an awkward aesthetic, and at twenty-six pounds, one can't really call it lightweight, though it is easy to assemble and disassemble. (Granted, these last few words have an ominous ring to them.) Kangaroo has a few competitors, mostly overseas, where golf cars aren't allowed on courses, but the machines aren't cheap, residing somewhere in the four-hundred-to-seven-hundred-dollar range. In this corner-cutting world, they aren't a bad idea—though they're no substitute for real caddies. However, they won't talk back and will travel unattended up to one hundred yards.

Browning's "Master" golf cart is quite possibly the most deluxe model available. It comes replete with whitewall tires, hubcaps and white vinyl side stool.

Weighing about sixteen pounds, the Caddybag "Whole in One" folds up and fits neatly into your car trunk.

# CADDY

The idea for a combination golf bag/golf cart is hardly a new one—after all, the first golf carts were merely bags with small wheels attached. But the Caddybag "Whole in One" is a most reasonably evolved descendant of these archaic contraptions and actually functions quite well. Weighing in at a reasonable sixteen pounds, the Caddybag will fit in a car trunk handily, and the process of assembly is relatively easy. (In a few steps the cart frame and wheels are popped out of and back into the bag prior to and after each use.) The bag is big enough (8½ inches at the mouth) and the cart sturdy enough (galvanized steel) to make an attractive, functional package for the non-prestige-oriented golfer.

President Dwight D. Eisenhower's
Golf Cart

This Cart was used by President Eisenhower
at His Home in Gettysburg, Pennsylvania.

Donated By Mrs. Mamie Eisenhower

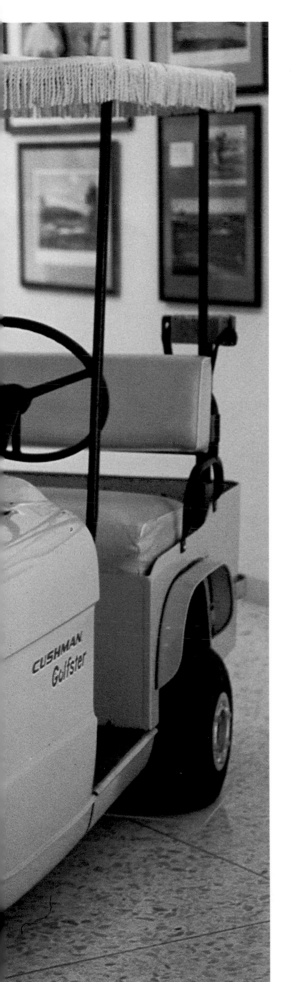

# GOLF CARS

*"He who have fastest cart never have to play bad lie." Mickey Mantle—Esquire, 1971*

With all due respect to "The Mick," golf "cars," not "carts," is the correct name for the motorized vehicles that carry clubs and golfers over hill and vale at just about every course, public or private, in America. The rental of these transports has become such a profitable sideline that most golf clubs could not stay in business without them.

The very first golf car was the "Arthritis Special," developed and patented in 1948 by a Texas oilman named R. J. Jackson. This machine—also called the "Half-Gone Special," after the inventor's advancing years—was a modified three-wheeled military utility vehicle, whose front-riding ferrying platform was replaced by a cast-iron park bench where golfers could ride (the driver rode behind on a small seat). Because of its smoke, noise and weight, this car and its gas-modeled successors had little future on the golf course.

In the mid-1950s, Cushman developed an electric car that quickly became the industry standard. (Harley Davidson's invention of the two-cycle engine brought the gas car back, though in far fewer numbers than electric.) With the golf boom of the past twenty-five years, the golf car's success in a car-conscious society was all but guaranteed. In thirty years' time, the number of golf cars in use on the nation's courses has grown to one million.

## EZ-GO

EZ-GO, the oldest and most successful outfit in the golf-car business, began as a tiny company in 1954. By 1956 they were producing electric cars; today they are the largest manufacturer of "utility" vehicles in the world.

Using an eight-horsepower engine, EZ-GO currently builds a solid, standard no-frills car that withstands the constant use (and abuse) of everyday course rental life. (The average golf car goes some 248 rounds per year at municipal courses.) Some of the heavy-duty features that add up to EZ-GO's durability and performance: helical axle differential reduces noise level; single, solenoid, self-adjusting controller demands less battery recharge; self-compensating hill brake eliminates linkage adjustments; multiple leaf-springed front end with hydraulic shocks provides a smooth ride; and rack-and-pinion steering gives precise handling. In short, all the accoutrements of a well-engineered machine.

Another nice aspect to EZ-GO cars is their simple design. With the company's success, they could easily opt for a top-shelf, high-tech streamlined look. Instead, they have retained a traditionally unpretentious industrial style with simple quiet tones that don't draw undue attention around the course.

An old Cushman golf car on display at the PGA Golf Hall of Fame.

The long-extinct,
three-wheel
Walker golf car
had a distinct
fifties look.

## EARLY BOMBS

Unfortunately, some of the first golf cars didn't stick around very long, mainly for lack of a market. Their unique early-fifties configurations would certainly turn a few heads on the course today.

The three-wheeled Walker "*Executive*" had a sleek post-Deco look that has to be among the hippest motor designs to come out of the golf world.

Advertisements for the Red-E Tractor Co.'s "*Fairway Sportster*" stressed "no tipping over," which, after seeing the prototype, could hardly have been reassuring. Looking more like a small tractor than anything else, this car seems too unwieldy to have adequately handled varying course terrains. An oversize muffler supposedly kept noise down and a tankful of gas was good for eighteen to twenty-seven holes.

The Joe-Be "*Caddymobile*" had the right idea, predating today's luxury golf cars. This three-wheeled vehicle had it all—running boards, an electrical outlet suggested for shaving or making coffee (just what you need on the golf course, right?) and a holder for a large lawn umbrella. 1955 price tag: $790.

The "*Eshelman Golf Car*" was a gasoline economy model of its day (1956). Ironically, Eshelman's ads stated that their models would make their electric competitors "as old-fashioned on the golf course as they are on the highway." It turned out the other way around.

# YAMAHA

For those who like to ride in style, Yamaha's "Sun Classic" is the ticket and a priccy one at that. At over $5,000, it just about approaches the price of some small economy cars. Actually, some of this golf car's features may be just as well geared for the streets as for the links.

Here are a few of the standard features that may help the golfer who must have everything negotiate a golf course: smoked windshield, self-canceling turn signals, electronic instrument panel, chromed wheels with whitewalls, high-beam headlights and a horn—this last should come in handy for speeding up a slow foursome in front. Set to travel around thirteen miles per hour, the Sun Classic can be hot-rodded up to thirty. AM-FM radio and plush carpeting are optional, and, yes, there is a space to put your golf clubs on the back.

# ELMCO

Not to be outdone by Rodney Dangerfield's outrageous arrival on the links in a well-known Lite beer commercial, Elmco, Inc., has come up with the ultimate in course transport—limited edition "cars of distinction." Built on aluminum chassis, Elmco's electric cruismobiles offer gold-plated bumper and grill, leather seats, shag carpeting, a beverage cooler and a sunroof. Available in two-tone, they'll only set you back $15,000 apiece.

There are over a million golf cars on US courses today, with no overnight trend toward walking in sight.

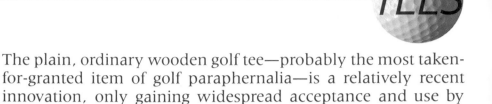

TEES

The plain, ordinary wooden golf tee—probably the most taken-for-granted item of golf paraphernalia—is a relatively recent innovation, only gaining widespread acceptance and use by the 1940s.

For centuries, golfers "teed up" for each new hole by stacking up little mounds of sand or dirt. By the 1890s, buckets of sand were usually furnished for this purpose at each teeing area. Small molds were expressly designed for forming tees with wet sand, and it was a caddy's job to carry these and properly shape the mound to the player's specifications.

In 1889, the first rubber-cup tee was patented in England. Different prototypes soon appeared in various metals; some had tassels for easy spotting, some had cord attachments.

William Lowell, a Maplewood, New Jersey, dentist, was the father of the standard wooden golf tee—an inventive feat that, as it affects golfers, should equal the creation of the wheel. Concerned that sand might be bad for his hands, Lowell came up with the first wooden-peg tee in 1922, something called the "Reddy Tee."

Today's traditionally shaped "arrow" tee is 2⅛ inches long,

Courtesy The Golf Works/©Randall D. Williams

Courtesy The Golf Works/©Randall D. Williams

and stamped from hardwood dowels, usually birch or maple. Painted, these tees will wholesale for a little over one cent apiece, provided you buy a minimum of one thousand (even cheaper by the fifty thousand) from a distributor or major golf manufacturer. For a slight extra charge, most companies offer personalized tees: "Joe's Bar & Grill," "Duffer's Anonymous," "Johnny Loves Judy," whatever.

Also available in wooden tees, from Eastern Golf Corporation, are cone-shaped "Carrot" tees and a new "Dart" tee, with a smaller head for alleged "minimum ball-area-to-surface contact." Eastern and others also offer rubber flange tees (very similar to the 1889 design) and plastic tripod tees—impossible to lose and good for hard ground.

Another new tee is TrueTee, a computer-designed plastic jobbie that will supposedly offer seventy-one percent less resistance than regular tees. The ball is propped up on three prongs that are made from Xenoy, a plastic alloy that is soft yet practically impossible to break. The idea here is that the ball will be hit *off* the tee not *out of* it, resulting in, you guessed it, more distance.

Courtesy The Golf Works/©Randall D. Williams

# GOLF GLOVES

*"I used to use three a round, but since I bought the company, I only use one."*
—Jack Nicklaus on MacGregor gloves, Golf Digest, *1983.*

Although never really catching on at the time, the golf glove was available in England as early as 1900. Even as late as 1940, most golfers eschewed gloves, especially professionals. (Real men don't wear gloves?) The first highly visible golfer to wear a glove was Sam Snead, and, perhaps from his lead, it became standard equipment by the late fifties. Today, there are only a handful of gloveless professionals on the tour and proportionally even fewer amateurs and hackers in their company.

## GIMMICK GLOVES

All the great pros will emphasize the importance of the hands and the grip to attaining a good golf game. No surprise really that someone would come up with an illegal glove to help you play better.

In 1966, Rod Campbell, a Pennsylvania driving-range pro, and Dr. Stanley K. Herberts, a Philadelphia optometrist, designed a golf glove guaranteed to add seventy-five yards to tee shots. The trick was to sew four ounces of buckshot into the back of the glove. The added weight would supposedly pull the hands down faster; the added hand speed would mean more distance. The problem was U.S.G.A. approval—or lack of it. Consequently, the glove hasn't been heard from since.

The currently available "Shotmaker" golf glove is intended to create an automatic proper grip. It's also advertised as "not for tournament" play, meaning illegal. For those who have trouble holding the club without its slipping or sliding around, the Shotmaker has a metal insert sewn into the palm which will insure proper alignment. Let your conscience be the guide.

Courtesy Foot-Joy Inc.

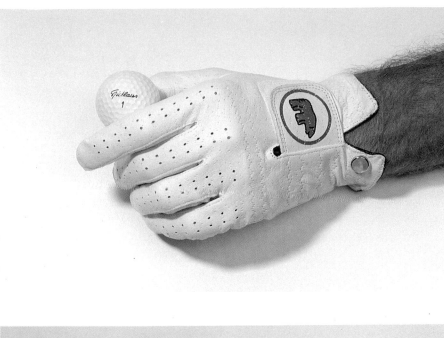

Courtesy MacGregor Golf Products

Courtesy MacGregor Golf Products

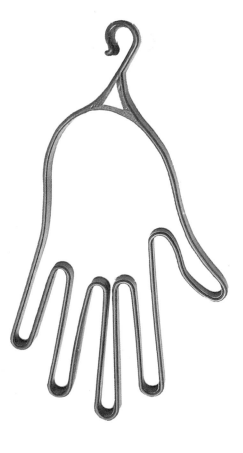

# FOOT-JOY

Foot-Joy is the most popular glove today, specifically the "Sta-Sof" model introduced in the early 1980s. Like most golf gloves, it is made of Ethiopian cabretta lambskin leather—known for its thinness, light weight and strength. The immediate sensation of a new cabretta leather glove is one of extreme "tackiness," which translates into good feel. Cabretta leather is also extremely soft and supple, but in this case the tanning process (Pittards of England) insures a high degree of water resistance, against both rain and perspiration. Foot-Joy's "Cooler" model golf glove is a warm-weather version, perforated all over for proper aeration.

# MACGREGOR

The five-dollar MacGregor "MacSuede" golf glove is not made of suede; it's nylon mesh on the back and garment-leather-reinforced on the palm, and it does kind of look like suede. But the MacSuede glove is a viable economic alternative to cabretta—twice as cheap and longer-lasting.

Machine-washable, the MacSuede gains in durability what it sacrifices in feel. Some players rapidly wear out golf gloves—especially the thin cabretta leather. Within a few rounds in humid weather, a $10-to-$15 glove can look like a shredded tissue. For these golfers, the MacSuede may be the answer if they can get over its polyester feel. At any rate, it's highly water-repellent.

A Reddy Tee (*below*) and an electronic Caddy Card are a few among a plethora of golf gadgets. One of the most traditional practice devices is the putting cup (*opposite page above*). The Swing Groover (*opposite page below*) helps you work on your swing without shagging balls. *Far right:* The Check-Go golf ball balancer finds every ball's center of gravity.

# GADGETRY

*"Do not be tempted to invest in a sample of each golfing invention as soon as it makes its appearance. If you do, you will only complicate and spoil your game—and encumber your locker with useless rubbish."*
—Harry Vardon, 1890s champion

First of all, let's say that there is no end to the amount of gadgets that have been and will continue to be created for the avaricious golf consumer, or for his generous relatives who will give him any golf-related gift, thinking it makes him happy. (It probably does.) With this in mind, let's proceed to the following items, while also keeping a good grip on golfing reality: They will not chop strokes off your game.

The **Check Go** is a little contraption that will balance your golf ball before you tee it up or before you putt. If you're confused, understand that the creation of this device is based on the premise that all golf balls are, however minutely, out of balance—a natural result of the manufacturing process. So you just pop your ball into the Check Go and, within seconds, the center of mass will be located, indicating where the ball should be struck for the truest roll. Aren't there some things we'd rather not know?

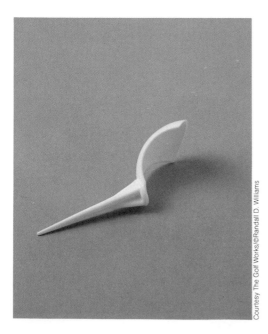

Courtesy The Golf Works/©Randall D. Williams

Courtesy Austad's

*Right:* A ball shag-ger holds up to eighty-five balls, saves back wear-and-tear. *Below:* A swing analyzer's monitor shows distance and di-rection, as well as details swing defi-ciencies. *Opposite page:* This old Sam Snead prac-tice mat helped golfers align feet according to club selection.

Courtesy The Golf Works/©Randall D. Williams

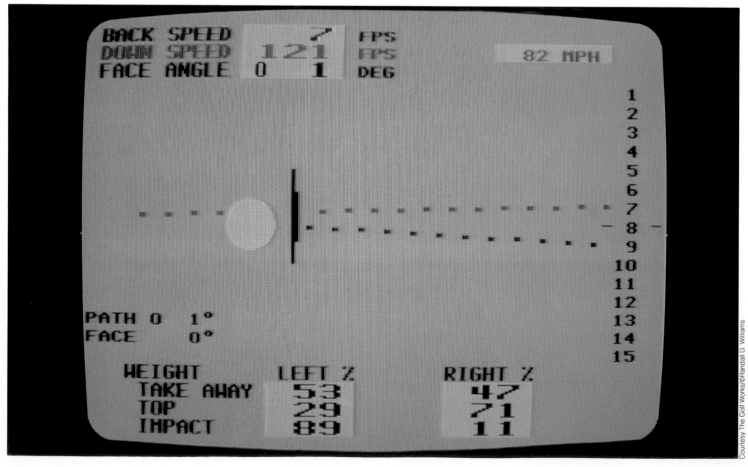

Courtesy The Golf Works/©Randall D. Williams

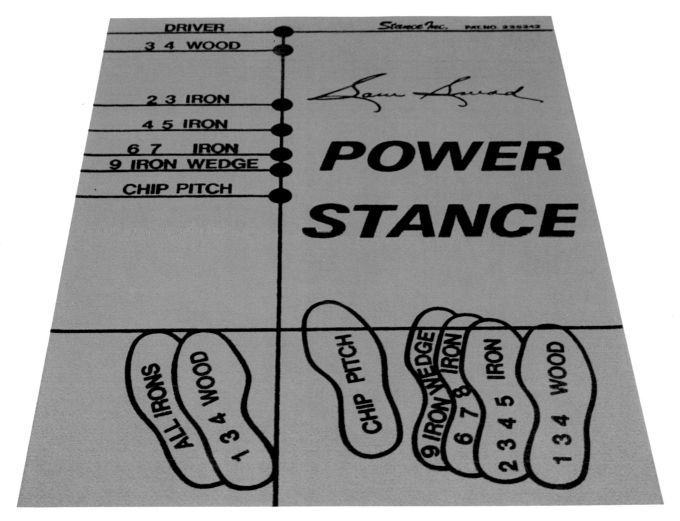

Macho golfers do not carry those extendable golf-ball retrievers, the idea being that they won't lose balls in water. Well, they will, and those who do carry the things invariably have larger used ball collections. The Austad Company offers three reasonably priced models, all under twenty dollars: the **Trap-it Retriever,** ten feet, with retracting pin that traps the ball; the **Basket Retriever,** ten to fifteen feet, with chromed wire heads that can pick up two balls at once; and the **Double Cup Retriever,** eighteen feet and fluorescent orange for easy spotting in murky water.

The **Deluxe Ball Shagger** is a traditional and worthwhile invention that will save backaches and add practice time. Holding up to eighty-five balls, the shagger picks up balls via a spring-clip system and sends them up the aluminum tube to a nylon bag where they're stored.

The **Rangefinder,** in one form or another, has been around for quite some time. It's also always been against the rules of golf, for those who care about small details. You simply are not allowed to use any device that will help you estimate yardage, which is what it does. By sighting the flagstick through a viewfinder and lining it up on a distance scale, the golfer figures his exact yardage to the pin. Any golfer who needs and can benefit from one of these things will probably find other ways to mess up his round.

# GOLF FASHIONS

*"Baffling late-life discovery. Golfers wear those awful clothes on purpose."*
—*Herb Caen*, San Francisco Chronicle

All right, let's get it out of the way to begin with: Golfers today, especially men, may play better than their predecessors, but they just don't cut it when compared to the sartorial splendor on the links of yesteryear. Look at pictures of old golfers, and you have to say, "What happened?" Well, for one thing, golfwear has become more comfortable.

It's hard to say when the change began. René Lacoste's creation of the knit "tennis" shirt, which generically has become commonly known as the golf shirt, help to a large extent, but it's safe to say that the pros set the trends all along. Walter Hagen, Bobby Jones, Gene Sarazen, et al. are of course remembered for knickers, or plus fours, but a closer look reveals a splendid attention to detail, from the ties and bow ties, to the starched collars, to the sleeveless sweaters, to the cuff links, to the Argyles, all the way down to the two-tone shoes.

Bobby Jones and Ross Somerville in standard attire at the 1930 National Amateur Championship. *Below left:* Gary Player in his traditional black from years past. *Below right:* Jimmy Demaret in seniors competition wearing a newer version of traditional knickers.

Jimmy Demaret helped the transition along by bringing his wild, self-designed, color-splotched outfits to the tour in the 1940s (to unnerve opponents, some said). In the fifties, the trend veered toward comfort, yet golfers retained the elegance of pleated, sharply creased pants and alpaca sweaters. Greats like Hogan, Nelson and Snead were more identifiable by their hats than anything else.

In the sixties, Arnold Palmer may have helped the casual look along, with his burly athletic demeanor. After a couple of holes, he'd be sweating, shirt out, glove hanging from his back pocket. Then a guy like Doug Sanders comes along and all the golf world calls him a fashion plate for his purple, magenta or chartreuse shoes that match his Sansabelt pants and polyester shirts. Yuck.

## MAIL ORDER

There's a silly taboo around many private clubs: You don't buy your equipment in discount houses or by mail order, where you can get it a lot cheaper—you buy from the club pro, whose livelihood depends on your business. Well, aside from personal club-fitting and advice, there's really no need to be paying twice as much as necessary, anywhere. Mail-order houses have become very big and their bargain prices make even sporting-goods stores seem like Tiffany's. All of the following offer free catalogues:

**AUSTAD'S** (800) 843-6828—clubs, clothing, balls, miscellaneous.
**THE BOOKLEGGER** (800) 262-1556—books, videos
**COMPETITIVE EDGE GOLF** (800) 334-0854—clubs, gadgetry
**EASTERN GOLF CORPORATION** (800) 482-7200—course mainte-nance, miniature golf, driving-range equipment.
**EDWIN WATTS GOLF SHOPS** (800) 874-0146—clubs
**GOLFSMART** (800) 637-3557—books, videos
**LAS VEGAS DISCOUNT GOLF** (800) 634-6743—clubs, shoes
**NEVADA BOB'S DISCOUNT GOLF** (800) 634-6202—clubs, shoes, balls, miscellaneous.
**OLD GOLF SHOP** (800) 227-8700—memorabilia, books, gift items

Today, nearly every professional golfer endorses some sort of clothing line. Whether or not a bill is necessary to keep the sun out of the eyes, the logo atop will pay some bills. Larry Mize's three-shades-of-purple shirt is still with us from his 1987 Masters win—would the guy really select that rag on the most important day of his life? If they couldn't sell it before that, they've probably moved a few since. Then there's Payne Stewart in the pink knickers. Funny, but you just don't see a lot of those down at the ol' club.

Ladies golfwear has evolved in much the same manner, fortunately toward comfort. Turn-of-the-century modes had women covering all flesh but the hands and face. It's a wonder they could swing, with the bustles, high collars and all. Gradually, hemlines went north, and shorts even became permissible—in some cases only under the threat of lawsuit.

So maybe some of us don't care for the garish colors, the goofy-looking pants and all the logos on golf clothes. (Try and find a soft, one-hundred-percent-cotton knit shirt with no ad on it.) Still, on a hot day modern golfwear beats playing with tweeds, a tie and long socks—even if it doesn't look as good.

*Opposite page:* Arnie, with dangling glove in back pocket, is one of the most popular golfers of all time. *Below:* The always-elegant Don January and Sam Snead, whose trademark was the casual straw hat.

©Bob Daemmrich

## SHIRTS

In the form of the soft and flexible cotton short-sleeved shirt, "casual" wear came to us via the golf tour. It was a Frenchman who put the alligator on, but it was golfers who sold the shirts worldwide.

Today's well-known brands—**Aureus, Mark Scot, Lacoste, La Mode,** etc.—are pretty much the same thing all around. Most manufacturers offer some models in one hundred percent cotton, and why take anything else, except maybe for shrinkage? New "mercerized" cotton adds sheen and strength, but you pay the price in how it feels on the skin. Also, non-buckling, hard-contoured collars are in, even if they do look like they scrape the neck. Obviously, we're still not quite there on this comfort thing or we'd all just be wearing T-shirts.

## PANTS

The question on golf pants should be: Why would anyone wear something on the golf course they wouldn't be caught dead in anywhere else? A quick glance around the racks of any pro shop makes it apparent that golf-apparel manufacturers don't care a whit about the answer.

Again, golf pants are primarily geared for comfort. **Sansabelt** slacks are the most popular, having been around, virtually unchanged, since 1957. They're the ones with the triple-stretch elastic waistband that moves with the wearer. Sansabelt's success stems largely from the ability to work with, and around, the midriff bulge. Once available only in polyesters, they can be found today in a variety of cottons, linens and poplins.

## KNICKERS

Seen primarily on television, as worn by Billy Casper and Payne Stewart, plus fours were once de rigueur on the course. (The term "plus four" indicates a bloused knicker that falls four inches lower than normal.)

The **T. Barry Knicker Co.** version is worn by Casper, Bob Hope and Claude Akins, among others, and is available in linen, gabardine and flannel. T. Barry also offers matching Argyle sweater-sock sets and an outrageous knickered tuxedo. **Head** showcases the hideous white-pink-and-red knickers worn by Payne Stewart, if hardly anyone else. **Austad's** mail order has affordable "summer-weight" tartan-plaid knickers of sixty-five percent polyester, for those who aren't tradition-bound.

*Far left:* The "polo" shirt was designed by a Frenchman and put on the map by golfers. *Center:* Cold-weather attire permits play in any weather. *Above:* "Plus fours" were once *de rigueur* on the golf course; today, they're making a mild comeback.

*Below:* The golf shoe originated in late nineteenth century Britain, when golfers screwed hobnails into the soles of their boots. *Opposite page:* Three different models of Footjoys.

## SHOES

In the late nineteenth century, some British golfers screwed hobnails into the soles of their boots, a less than comfortable solution to loss of traction. These, and the aluminum spikes used in the trenches of World War I by German soldiers, were the forerunners to the modern golf shoe that first appeared in the early twentieth century.

**Foot-Joy** dominates golf's shoe market, boosted by eighty-five percent wear on the pro tour. Their best-known product is the "Classic," a simple, washable calfskin shoe that comes in a variety of styles and colors. Their other, more lightweight styles may gain in comfort what they lose in support, and are also waterproof. For those unafraid or unaware of social stigmas, the "Exotics" collection offers lizard and alligator hides.

**Fore Ltd.** may be the most sylish golf shoes going, if at the expense of some of nature's finest. These shoes aren't cheap ($400-$1200); they come in different styles of calfskin, trimmed with a choice of python, shark, boa, lizard, crocodile, ostrich or elephant skin. Yikes! Fore also innovated the brass toeplate (as worn by Payne Stewart), which is supposed to help maintain balance.

## RAINWEAR

Top of the line in this department is the **Jack Nicklaus Goretex** outfit, made from a space-age fabric with billions of microscopic pores per square inch. This waterproofing system blocks water, while allowing body heat to escape. It's also lightweight, allows total freedom of movement and can cost as much as a cheap set of clubs ($150-$200).

A reasonable alternative to Goretex (and one-fourth the price) is the **Briarcliff** rain suit, with pockets and zippered cuffs to ease over spikes. **Austad's** mail order has a rain suit for as little as thirteen dollars.

©Keith Glasgow

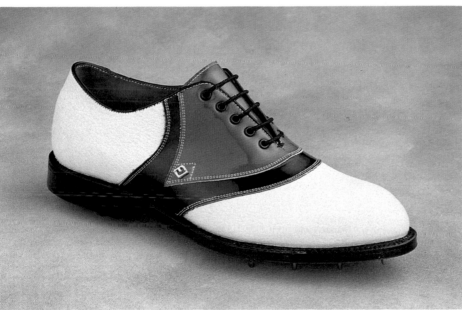

SECTION II
*Courses, Resorts and Clubs*

Scotland is the undisputed home of golf, and the most stately and famous of all Scottish golf courses is St. Andrews (*opposite page and below*). Golf has been played here in some form or another since the middle of the fifteenth century.

It's safe to say that without a Scotland there would have been no golf—"wouldna' been nae gawf." Crude and basic compared to the manicured terrains we know today, the very first courses evolved over centuries of straddling the complimentary topography of seaside northern Scotland. The term "links" is generally used to categorize all early (and contemporary) sand and windswept seaside courses, but, more specifically, the earliest "linksland" consisted of rich alluvial deposits that collected over sand dunes along river estuaries. It was thus that the game originated along the Firths of Eden, Tay and Forth, near Edinburgh, off the North Sea.

Designed by nature, these earliest courses were also naturally maintained. The sand beneath the soil made for excellent drainage, and grazing sheep or wild game kept the grass mowed. At first there was no standard number of holes—golfers simply played one direction as far as they could, then played their way back.

The most famous of the early courses was St. Andrews, where golf existed in some form or another as far back as the mid-1400s. Every aspect of the game can trace roots to the "Old Course," forever golfdom's Mecca. Originally, the layout consisted of twenty-two holes with only twelve putting areas, ten of which were used twice ("out," then back "in"), with the remaining two played once apiece, as the eleventh and closing holes. It was in 1764 that the model for "modern" golf was

born, when the Society of St. Andrews Golfers decided to consolidate the first four holes into two long ones. This meant two less holes in each direction, leaving a total of eighteen, the standard ever since.

While there were only seventeen golf courses in Scotland by 1857, traveling Scots had already begun to introduce their ancient game all over the world. It was at Blackheath in 1608 that the game first appeared in England, where, by 1888, there were seventy-three courses. A golf club existed in South Carolina as early as 1786, one in Calcutta by 1829, one atop the Pyrenees in France in 1856 and five in Canada by 1876.

Today, there are approximately 21,500 worldwide facilities at which to play golf. The United States has thirteen thousand courses to accommodate (or at least try to) the twenty million American golfers. Forty percent of these are private clubs. Yankee hackers don't really have it so bad when contrasted with Japan's ten million players, who have a mere fourteen hundred courses—most are not available to the hoi polloi.

The following pages highlight some of the most attractive, most difficult and most unique courses; also featured are choice resorts and municipal courses. Some are terribly exclusive or expensive, some quite difficult to get to. But for every Augusta or Pine Valley that too few of us will ever get near, much less play, there is Pebble Beach, Pinehurst, even the hallowed turf of St. Andrews—all accessible to the lousiest of linksmen.

# THE BEST

Any grouping of "best" golf courses in the world could also be termed "most difficult," "most famous" or "most beautiful," without making many changes. Whether one can enjoy a probable round of over one hundred at Augusta National—should one be fortunate enough to have an in for an invite—is debatable; that the springtime flora is exhilarating, that the course is among the ten "greatest," are not. Rating ten or so best courses is much easier than a top one hundred. The cream of golf courses has risen to the top so visibly in golfing history that most top-ten lists are practically identical. Here then, in no particular order, are ten of the very best golf courses.

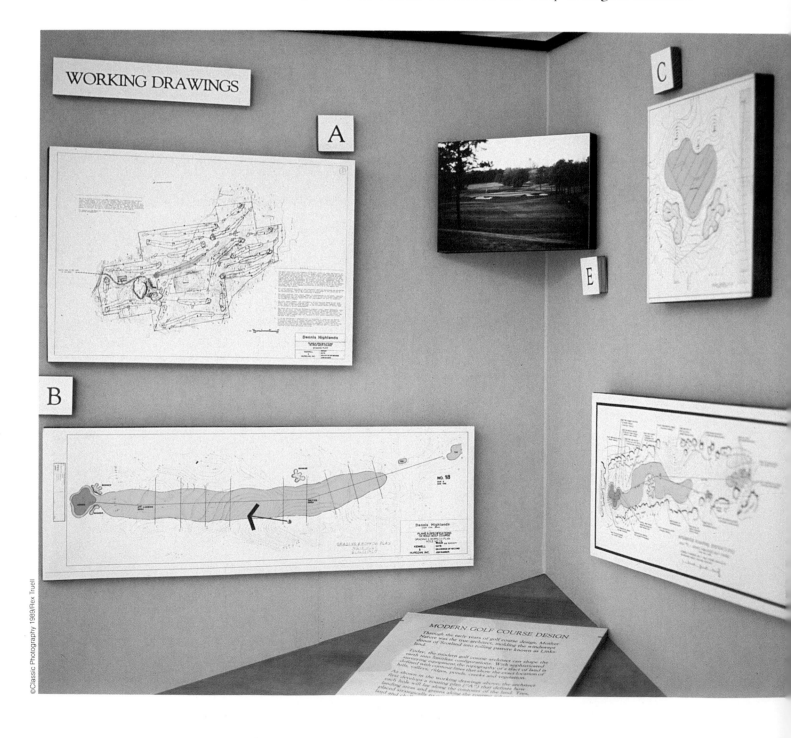

©Keith Glasgow

# ST. ANDREWS

St. Andrews, Scotland

Steeped in tradition, hallowed and sacrosanct, birthplace of golf, host of twenty-two British Opens, St. Andrews remains democratically open to the common hacker. For the dedicated traveler, it's not much more complicated than attending mass at Chartres—and a not altogether different experience.

Cradled between the North Sea and a quaint old town, the "Old Course" carved itself from the sand-scape over four centuries. Around 1850, a committee decided to widen the narrow fairways by replacing the adjacent heather crops with turf. This changed the label of "penal" design to "strategic"—offering both a more hazardous, direct route for the bold player, and a longer, indirect route for the safe player. Either way, blind hazards and fearsome bunkers rule the layout.

Those wishing to play the "Old Course" (there are three other less challenging seaside courses at St. Andrews) had best book long in advance for summer dates. They don't give wind checks, but the post-round malt Scotches can soothe even the most gale-ruffled of golfing egos.

*Opposite page:* Diagrams, maps and drawings of famous courses (and holes) line the walls of the U.S.G.A.'s Golf House. *Above:* The ancient clubhouse in the background of the birthplace of golf: St. Andrews in Scotland.

## ARCHITECTS

In 1848, club and ballmaker Allen Robertson widened the fairways at St. Andrews. Aside from pleasing the local hackers, this was significant in that it was the first golf-course architecture of any sort. Since then, millions upon millions of acres of land have been speculated, surveyed, dug up, plowed over, sodded, land-scaped, gulleyed, rearranged, designed and bulldozed—all in the name of golf-course architecture.

The first course architects were usually either club professionals with a keen understanding of the game and an eye for adaptable terrain, or dilettantes with visions of grand designs over which they and their cohorts could then enjoy the game. It wasn't until a few decades ago that course architecture became a serious profession. Today, the field has become cluttered with playing professionals. Everybody and his brother is designing a course, which isn't to belittle the fine efforts of the likes of Arnold Palmer, Tom Watson and Jack Nicklaus. The following five masters have and will continue to influence all course designers.

### PETE DYE

Because of his radical, and some-times exceedingly penal, course designs, Pete Dye has been called a sadist, among other unprintables. His favorite answer is, "Golf wasn't meant to be fair."

Dye is the creator of the first TPC course at Sawgrass, a course that typifies his concept of "target golf"—landing areas for drives, water on every hole and small greens with rolling contours. The course is also the first of the "stadium" layouts, with steep embankments surrounding the narrow fairways for spectating. Purists call it "Star Wars golf, designed by Darth Vader."

The fabled 16th at Augusta. A painting of the hole by Dwight D. Eisenhower hangs in the Golf House museum. This beautiful course, the "Cathedral in the Pines," is the home of the Masters.

# AUGUSTA NATIONAL
Augusta, Georgia

*"The closest thing to heaven for a golfer, and just about as difficult to get into."*
—*Joe Gershwiler* San Francisco Examiner, *1982.*

In 1932, Bobby Jones, the ruling sovereign of golf, opened Augusta National, his personal playground and dream course. Sculpted from a Georgia arboretum and co-designed by renowned course architect Alister Mackenzie, Augusta remains as pastoral as it is exacting, but it was for tournament golf that it was essentially created.

For spectators at the Masters, the "Cathedral in the Pines" provides great viewing from hillsides surrounding the greens. For players, the contours of the course are geared to competitive golf: broad fairways lined with tall Georgia pines; large, undulating greens cut to marble smoothness; deceivingly few yet expertly placed bunkers; and two streams that snake in and out of play.

Via Masters' telecasts, millions of us return to Augusta each April—to the blooming azaleas and dogwoods, to the idyllic sixteenth over water, to our own sub-par fantasy rounds in the pines. There may be some comfort in knowing that even the three hundred or so members can't always tee up—to preserve the course, play is prohibited during the summer months. Best bet for getting on: Get to know someone on staff, or, better yet, become a caddie, since Mondays are "caddies' days."

# PINE VALLEY
Clementon, New Jersey

*"Hell, I don't need to know where the green is; where's the golf course?"*
—*Babe Ruth, playing Pine Valley.*

Although generally regarded as the world's most difficult course, Pine Valley shouldn't be judged by its sand alone. After all, the entire course is fashioned from a sandy wasteland twenty miles southeast of Philadelphia. Players who mishit basic tee or fairway shots will find themselves in some sort of annoying sand or scrubland, but them ain't traps. Traps—like the eight-foot-deep monstrosity affectionately nicknamed the "Devil's hole"—are found near greens. Because of its premium on perfect shot placement, pros love this course, but few will ever play it. The U.S.G.A. would love to have an Open here, but the reclusive nature of this club would never allow it. Golf is serious, private business at Pine Valley, a place where the club superintendent has a tattoo of the first hole on his forearm.

*Opposite page and right:* The wind swept links of Ballybunion. *Below:* The famous "church pew" at Oakmont.

# BALLYBUNION

Ballybunion, Ireland

It is entirely fitting that an eleventh-century Gaelic cemetery skirts the right side of Ballybunion's first fairway, since a large water hazard, the Atlantic, serves as a slicer's graveyard for most of the course. Actually, the first few holes on what has to be the rawest and most rustic of links courses are relatively (and literally) a breeze. From the seventh (a windblown, 448 yard par four) on, things get rough, usually in correlation to the elements. It's not uncommon to go through a year's worth of seasons in a round. Rainwear is essential, but an umbrella is practically useless, since the wind blows the rain sideways into a fine mist that comes at the golfer from every direction. On an atypically sunny day, Tom Watson once shot a vacationing seventy-two, but die-hard locals will forever begrudge him the fair weather, maintaining that he never played the "real" course. Although the club is a private one with members, play is unrestricted to the visiting stout of heart.

# OAKMONT

Oakmont, Pennsylvania

*"A shot poorly played should be a shot irrevocably lost."*
— *William C. Fownes, Oakmont architect.*

Fownes wasn't kidding, and to prove it he redesigned the links-type course that his father had built in 1903 overlooking the Allegheny River. He lengthened holes, shortened par, canted greens, even dug ditches in the rough. But, most of all, he added sand—over 220 bunkers, of which 190 remain. By the time he was finished, Oakmont epitomized his credo, as well as the penal style of architecture.

Host to to five U.S. Opens, Oakmont is not a beautiful course; there are few trees, there is no water, and the layout is bisected by the Pennsylvania Turnpike. But there is a perverse beauty to the mazelike trap configurations, particularly the "Church Pews" at the third and fourth holes—provided one doesn't attend services. The greens, rolled and manicured to 3/32nds of an inch, are possibly the fastest in the world, but lovely as well. Johnny Miller once took Oakmont by the throat to win an Open with a closing sixty-three, but the real question should be, do the members actually enjoy this course?

©Brian Morgan

©Brian Morgan

## ALISTER MACKENZIE

Had Alister Mackenzie not given up his English medical practice for course design, we would never have been blessed with Pebble Beach, Cypress Point or Augusta, three of the greatest courses ever built.

Even as a mediocre player, Mackenzie extolled the therapeutic values of the game, as well as the belief that it could increase "the virility and prosperity of a nation." His design principles were based on imitating natural undulations of the earth so as to retain principles of harmony and balance. He also believed in making holes appear more difficult than they actually were so that golfers might experience the thrill of accomplishing the seemingly impossible. Here! Here!

# PEBBLE BEACH–CYPRESS POINT

Pebble Beach, California

*"Cypress Point—the looks of Christie Brinkley, the tenderness of Tokyo Rose."*
—Bob Hope, Golf Magazine, 1983.

That two of the world's most spectacular courses should lie within a mile of each other is a testament to the suitability of seaside golf and to the eyes of those who foresaw the layout for a linkstyle garden of Eden.

Actually, Pebble Beach is not strictly a links course, since it rests on bluffs overlooking Carmel Bay. The designers, two local amateurs, left existing terrain practically untouched and routed a combination of inland and seaside turf to dramatic effect. One stretch of seven holes along the Pacific Ocean is panoramically detrimental to concentration. Pebble Beach is and has always been a resort open to everyone, with greens fees as elevated as the greens. Anyone who's ever dined in a four-star restaurant shouldn't be deterred. This is better.

Cypress Point is a private golf course of majestic design by Alister Mackenzie. The sixteenth is perhaps the most photographed, best-known hole in America. A 220 yard par three that carries over the pounding Pacific, it is at once breathtaking and near impossible. Thanks to its strategic design, a player can choose to play off the tee to a larger and closer expanse of ground, then try and chip up for par. In the television ads, the guy always takes the bold route and soars his ball safely to the green. In real life, such a shot usually sends the ball bouncing into the raging surf one hundred yards below.

*Below:* The heart-stopping, par three 16th at Cypress Point—play safe to the left, or go for it over the rocks on the right.
*Opposite page:* The seventh at Pebble Beach. With views like this, how can anybody play golf?

©J. Zimmerman/FPG International

## DONALD ROSS

Considered by many to be the all-time greatest, Ross was certainly the most prolific of course architects. Having moved to the States from Scotland, he had over three thousand men building his courses at the peak of his career in 1925.

His most famous designs are the Pinehurst courses in North Carolina, distinguished by his sculptured putting greens, all molded into existing terrain—their sites often put a premium on short recoveries.

*Below:* The club-house at Winged Foot. *Right:* Pinehurst No. 2.

---

## ROBERT TRENT JONES

*"Golf should be a fair test. If the average golfer shoots 90, he'll be comfortable. If he shoots 120, he'll want to give up the game."* —R. T. Jones,
The New York Times
*1986*

Jones, who has designed over 450 courses nationwide, is considered the first bona-fide course designer (until then, others came from other fields), even creating a major of "golf architecture." at Cornell University.

Jones is a traditionalist, drawing from the great Scottish courses, and believing that nature should not be overly tampered with. His trademark is the elevated, plateaued green, all the more difficult for a ball to hold. As far as philosophy, Jones is disgruntled with the high-tech advances in equipment and balls, which may be why he makes every successive course a bit harder.

# ROYAL COUNTY DOWN

Newcastle, Northern Ireland

*"If you can see the Mourne Mountains, it's going to rain; if you can't see them, it's raining."*
—Local saying.

A stranger playing the front nine at County Down could be forgiven for wandering from the game (if not the wind-buffed course). The valleys of lush fairways framed by ridges of giant sand dunes and the backdrop of the purplish Mourne Mountains could be a visually disconcerting combo. Tough enough to play golf here, but commune with nature as well? Either way, a glorious experience.

In a land of egalitarian golf, Royal County Down is considered a bit starchy as a club; inquiries should be made through the club secretary. Tread lightly, go heavy on the respect.

# MUIRFIELD

Muirfield, Scotland

Golf purists like to rate Muirfield the No. 1 course in the world. They often refer to its straightforward, honest qualities and to its "fairness," but would this apply to most of us? The first hole is a 449-yard dogleg par four into the wind—is this a fair way to start a round? Ben Crenshaw says that the contours of the course tell you from each tee exactly where to hit the ball. Great. Now all you have to do is do it.

True fairness for all can be found in the routing—the first nine running a clockwise circle, the back nine a counterclockwise circle inside the first. But within the two loops holes are grouped in clusters of threes, each in a different direction. This means one never has to play two holes in a row into the wind.

Muirfield, officially named the Honorable Company of Edinburgh Golfers, dates back to 1744; it is the world's oldest golf club. Visitors must apply to play there well in advance, supplied with letters of introduction from presidents of their own clubs. Without a good word from the top, their chances are nil.

©Keith Glasgow

©Classic Photography 1989/Rex Truell

# PINEHURST NO. 2

Pinehurst, North Carolina

There are thirty-four golf courses nestled in the sand pines around Pine-hurst, North Carolina, a town of 3,000 inhabitants of whom 2,999 suppos-edly play golf. One of the great golf complexes of the world is the Pinehurst Country Club, comprising seven courses, the most famous being No. 2.

Pinehurst No. 2 was designed (and redesigned several times) by Donald Ross, a Scotsman who was the club pro. (Ross went on to become the most prolific—some say greatest—golf architect of all time, leaving his imprint all over America in the twenties and thirties.) No. 2 is a course of subtle difficulty: the fairways are wide, but often bordered by large areas of hardpan sand or pine groves; greens are small and sloped—try and avoid a solitary sand trap and you may find a greenside gully.

Reservations for tee times at Pinehurst Country Club courses are needed sixty days in advance, except during the "shoulder" season of early spring and late fall, when package rates for golf and hotel are surprisingly reason-able. The other courses at the Pinehurst Country Club are all quite beautiful and challenging, but No. 2 is both the most difficult and the most expensive (twenty dollar surcharge), which, naturally, makes it the most crowded.

## ALBERT WARREN TILLINGHAST

"Tillie the Terror" was a sportsman who hadn't done an honest day's work in his life, until, at the age of thirty-two, he transformed the family farm into a golf course. From there, he went on to form a design-and-construction firm that built some of the finest courses in the world, in-cluding Winged Foot and Baltusrol, two fabled U.S. Open layouts. His style was to design courses on the spot, alternately sipping from a flask and shouting orders. He is also cred-ited for coining the term "birdie," for one under par.

# COUNTRY CLUBS

In Japan, where golf is popular and land is at a premium, memberships to country clubs are traded on the stock exchange. Here are a few of the lucky ones at a country club in Tokyo. *Opposite page:* A double-tiered Japanese range at twilight; even driving ranges have waiting lists in Japan.

As far as golf goes, country clubs have a bad rap. For sure, snootiness, exclusivity and discrimination are not inappropriate terms when discussing the blue-blooded country-club tradition. Also, there is a peripheral social scene to private clubs that has little to do with the lure of the links. But, for pure golf, who wouldn't rather play with no waiting time on the lush, well-manicured turf of a private course? The sad fact is, most of us don't have the connections or the money to be able to enjoy the game in such a manner.

Initiation fees at country clubs in the New York City area, for example, will average from five thousand to seven thousand dollars, with annual dues coming in around three thousand dollars—this without counting drinks, food, social functions, etc. These figures (from a 1987 Metropolitan Golf Association survey of seventy-two clubs) will vary nationwide, but membership to "better" clubs can stretch more than fifty thousand dollars in some areas (most notably the West Coast)—some clubs even have yearly *assessed* dues! Ouch.

The U.S.G.A., ruling body of American Golf, was formed in 1894 by five of the very first private golf clubs: The Country Club, St. Andrews Golf Club, Newport Country Club, Shinnecock Hills Golf Club and the Chicago Golf Club. For a representative look at the highest echelons of country-club golf, we need look no further than this venerable quintet. Things haven't changed much since 1900 at each club, where tradition is still a very big theme, as it probably was back then.

## JAPAN GOLF

One needn't travel to Japan to know how obsessed with golf the entire country is. One need only see the smiling hordes of happy Japanese visitors that descend on our courses each summer. Know why they're so happy? Because back home most of them don't get to play—ever.

In 1987, a record $3.57 million was offered for a membership at the exclusive Koganei Country Club. Yet even at that bullish price (memberships at many clubs are brokered on the Tokyo Stock Exchange) no member was willing to sell. The average prices for joining clubs are back down—anywhere from $100,000 to $1 million for most clubs—but investors still sometimes purchase memberships for sheer speculation alone, driving the price of golf up, all the way down to greens fees on public courses (around a hundred dollars). Japan reportedly has twelve million golfers (or would-bes, anyway), with only 1400 courses, most private. With the cost of land so high, and with space at such a premium, there just isn't any place left for hackers except the driving ranges, and that's where most people "play," often waiting up to two hours and paying twenty-five cents a ball for the privilege of hitting a few drives.

## ESTATE GOLF

There are a few well-to-do hackers who have no use for private clubs, though this doesn't mean you'll see them down at the local public links. No, some people like to play in total privacy—like, nobody else on the course. What to do but build your own golf course?

Needing exercise, John D. Rockefeller took up golf in 1898 and built Potantico Hills, the oldest of "estate" courses. In the 1960s the family had the entire course renovated by Robert Trent Jones—replete with an occasional view of the Hudson River down below.

Walter Annenberg, businessman and former ambassador, has two such spreads: one functional three-green course in Pennsylvania and a stupendous six-thousand-yard layout in Palm Springs. Willie Nelson, Donald Trump and John Galbraith are a few other recognizable names among private course owners, but since the whole point of this game is privacy, there's no way to know how many of these places exist.

A six-green layout spread over forty acres, with three separate teeing areas for each, will cost between one and one and a half million dollars, land not included. Add on about seventy-five thousand dollars a year for maintenance. All right, so it ain't cheap. But can you imagine no tee times, no waiting for the creeps in front, no perverse pin placements? No rough, no hazards, for that matter, if you like. Could be golf heaven.

## ST. ANDREWS

Hastings-on-Hudson, New York

Striving for recognition as the birthplace of American golf (hotly contested between three or four clubs), St. Andrews can at the very least claim being the first country club where golf was officially played on a course. This occured in 1888, when a Scot named John Reid organized a group of five Yonkers, New York, gentlemen to build nine holes. They called themselves "St. Andrews," after the famous Scottish course. Within a few short years, the clubhouse at St. Andrews was a meeting place for the titans of industry. It was here that Charles Schwab created U.S. Steel by convincing Andrew Carnegie to sell out to J. P. Morgan. For all its austere roots, St. Andrews today is pleasantly free of stuffiness, with a relatively affordable membership charge of five thousand dollars (four thousand dues). The golfing is quite hilly, but the classic surroundings are warm and comfortable.

## THE COUNTRY CLUB

Brookline, Massachusetts

The Country Club, yes, *The*—that's what they go by—was the first of its namesake ever formed. But golf was not the primary focus when The Country Club opened in 1882. "The general idea," as stated in the original prospectus, "is to have a comfortable clubhouse...bedrooms, a simple restaurant, bowling alley, lawn tennis grounds...race meetings and occasionally music in the afternoon." A few years later, the princely sum of fifty dollars was appropriated for six golf holes, later extended to eighteen in 1910. (The racetrack still stands off to the side of the first hole.) Francis Ouimet, a twenty-year-old former caddie from the Club, gave American golf a great boost when he won the U.S. Open at Brookline in 1913, besting Vardon and Ray, two British immortals, in a playoff. To commemorate his win, the tournament was held fifty years later at The Country Club, in 1953, then again twenty-five years later, in 1988. Though far from the top shelf of U.S. Open courses, it has character, and, of course, it has that name.

©Brian Morgan

©Bill Wrenn

*Left:* Established in 1888, the American St. Andrews is the disputed birth-place of golf in the United States. *Below:* The club-house at St. An-drews, in the style of the archetypical English country inn.

*Opposite page:*
Newport Country
Club—the old
stone walls are
gone from across
the fairways.
*Right:* Shinnecock
Hills, host to the
1986 US Open,
closely resembles
the Scottish links
courses.

©Bill Wrenn

THE TEN TOUGHEST NORTH
AMERICAN CLUBS
(for nonmembers)

Augusta National Golf Club
*Augusta, Georgia*

Burning Tree Club
*Bethesda, Maryland*

Chevy Chase Club
*Chevy Chase, Maryland*

Cypress Point Club
*Pebble Beach, California*

Fisher's Island Golf Club
*Fisher's Island, New York*

Jupiter Island Club
*Hobe Sound, Florida*

Los Angeles Country Club
*Los Angeles, California*

Old Elm Club
*Fort Sheridan, Illinois*

Pine Valley Golf Club
*Clementon, New Jersey*

Toronto Golf Club
*Toronto, Ontario*

# TORONTO GOLF CLUB

Port Credit, Ontario

The Toronto Golf Club is one of the oldest and most exclusive Country Clubs in Canada. Designed in 1915 by renowned architect Harry Colt, this stunning, "members-only" course attempts to exist in virtual obscurity. It is an English-styled golf course with rolling hills and deep valleys that make accuracy a must. One of the most beautiful and unique aspects of this course is the abundance of large, mature trees that line every hole. This is a course that was designed to compliment the landscape, and not cut into it.

# GLEN ABBEY

Oakville, Ontario

Located in Oakville, Ontario, Glen Abbey is one of the finest and most famous courses in Canada. Jack Nicklaus designed this course in 1976—the first course that the "Golden Bear" designed on his own—since then it has become the home of the Canadian Open. The 14th Hole is rated one of the top eighteen toughest holes on the PGA Tour. This 426-yard, dogleg-right hole is guarded by a river that snakes through the fairway, making a decent drive a must. The second shot is at-least a 3–iron to the green. This is definitely not a hole for the faint of heart.

# NEWPORT COUNTRY CLUB

Newport, Rhode Island

Site of the first U.S. Open, in 1895, the Newport Country Club at that time had stone walls that straddled the fairways. These were thought to be "splendid" hazards by some members, if not by Charles Blair McDonald, great golfer and course architect of the day. The visiting McDonald lost an important challenge match by one stroke when he was penalized two strokes after his ball lodged itself under a wall. Anyway, the course was later redone—minus the stone walls—in superlative fashion.

# SHINNECOCK HILLS

Southhampton, New York

The ultimate links-style layout and the closest thing to Scottish courses this side of the Atlantic, Shinnecock is also the ultimate golf club. The original course was built in 1891, overlooking Great Peconic Bay on the South Fork of eastern Long Island, and was expanded before hosting the second U.S. Open in 1896. Like many of the great Scottish links, the course can be extremely difficult when the ocean breeze kicks up. Jack Nicklaus and several other pros found that out on the first day of the 1986 Open, when the wind howled and the scores soared. Renowned architect Stanford White designed the clubhouse, America's first. Shinnecock was also the first club to admit women (in their own right), and, as opposed to many Country Clubs, there are no restrictions as to when they can play.

# CHICAGO GOLF CLUB

Wheaton, Illinois

The Chicago Golf Club, home of the first eighteen-hole course in America, was organized in 1894 by Charles Blair Macdonald, about whom golf historian Herbert Warren Wind once wrote, "[He] was not 'Mr. American Golf,' though this was undoubtedly his lifelong ambition." Macdonald's fierce devotion to the game has been upheld gloriously at this magnificent inland course. "To us golf isn't a game, it's a way of life," a past president once told a member. Ben Crenshaw's sixty-two at Chicago will probably never be bested, but the members refuse to recognize it, since he took a "mulligan" (second drive) on the first hole.

# PUBLIC/MUNICIPAL GOLF

Some people, and they probably won't ever read this, still think that golf is the exclusive province of the very rich. Certainly there are parts of this book that do little to dispel that notion, and in some countries it does hold true. But as far as American Golf goes, most of us know better. We know that fifteen to twenty-five dollars (often less, if you walk) can buy a day's worth of communing with nature, kicking around a golf course anywhere across North America. And that's the way the majority of golfers play—"open" golf in the most democratic of surroundings. Public golf, people's golf.

Almost 2,000 of America's 13,000 courses are municipal—city, county, state park, etc. You won't find your shoes shined upon return to the clubhouse—assuming there even *is* a clubhouse—and your tee times can be about as dependable as a connecting flight in Atlanta. The greens are hopefully at least just that, green, and the condition of the fairways often varies according to water levels or the state of local funds. Your playing partners are as likely to be versed in golfing etiquette as Siberian refugees would be, and you might consider protective

©Brian Morgan

headgear for all the stray shots coming your way. But, hey, you're out on the course, the air is fresh, you're beating the ol' golf ball and, considering the cost of today's entertainment, this is a bargain.

Almost every municipality in North America has a course. Most golf nuts will know every place to play within a hundred-mile radius of where they live. For a complete rundown of where to play, call your county golf association or department of parks, or just use the Yellow Pages. The following is a cross-country cross section of public courses (mostly municipal)—all unique in their own right, yet all undeniably public.

The eighteenth (*opposite page*) and the sixth (*left*) at Chicago's Cog Hill No. 4. This course is widely considered one of the top twenty-five public courses and one of the top one hundred courses in North America.

## SAN FRANCISCO

**Harding Park**—City course, home of Ken Venturi, whose father was the club pro for many years.

**Golden Gate Park**—Another city course, in one of the world's most beautiful parks. Polo players seem to ignore the golfers and vice versa.

**Half Moon Bay**—Tough wind course, poor(er) man's Pebble Beach, overlooking Pacific.

Courtesy Cog Hill Golf Course

## CHICAGO

The Chicago Parks District ingeniously allows golfers to purchase advance tee times for city courses—there are six—at Ticketron outlets. Tops in charm is **Waveland,** with the Chicago skyline on one side and Lake Michigan on the other—each of the nine holes here is copied from a different famous course. New addition to Chicago Parks is **South Shore Country Club,** also fronting the lake. No electric golf cars allowed on Chicago's munis.

**Cog Hill**—A good drive out in the southwest burbs (Lemont) may be worth the four tough Cog Hill courses—the long and wooded No. 4 course is usually rated in the U.S. top 100.

*Right:* A watery grave for golf balls lies just in front of the narrow sixteenth green on Long Island's Montauk Downs. *Below:* The twelfth at Milwaukee's Brown Deer, a very, very long public course.

## CALGARY

**Shaganappi Point Golf Course**—An 18-hole, par 70 and a 9-hole, par 33, a surprisingly difficult little course despite the lack of sandtraps and water.

**McCall Lake**—A challenging links-type course with well-laid traps and 33 acres of water hazards.

## MILWAUKEE

**Brown Deer Golf Club**—County operated, over 7,000 yards, one of the country's best public courses.

## LONG ISLAND

**Bethpage State Park**—Four excellent eighteen-hole courses of graded difficulty. Black Course is the toughest.

**Montauk Downs State Park**—Gorgeous links-type course designed by Robert Trent Jones. Gusty winds, and severely bunkered, elevated greens, make this one of the most difficult public courses in the world.

## DALLAS

**Plano Municipal Golf Club**—Tough, woodsy layout, with a winding creek throughout.

## TORONTO

For those who can't sneak their way onto the course at the exclusive **Toronto Golf Club,** "People City" on lake Ontario boasts a fine selection of public courses. **Centennial Park Golf Centre** is a very public course that has a little something for everybody: an 18-hole, par 60 course; a driving range; and miniature golf for the younger set. In addition there is **Don Valley Golf Course,** one of Toronto's better public courses; the subway assessable **Denontia Park Golf Course;** the par 62 **Scarlett Woods Golf Course;** and the par 70 **Tam O'Shanter Golf Course.**

Courtesy Milwaukee County Parks Dept.

Courtesy New York State Office of Parks, Recreation & Historic Preservation

# DETROIT

**Palmer Park**—City playground where golf hustlers trim Motown execs. Has the feel of an outdoor poolroom.

# SAN DIEGO

**Torrey Pines**—Perhaps the best public course in the country. Site of the Andy Williams Open.

# PHOENIX

**Tatum Ranch**—Elevated tees and lush fairways in the middle of the otherwise preserved Sonoran Desert—cactus, ironwood, mesquite, Mexican poppies, sagebrush.

# EDMONTON

**Broadmoor Golf Course**—a 6216-yard, par 71 that is nestled among some of the finest homes in Sherwood Park.

**Golden West Golf Course**—A challenging course that has recently been rebuilt. A lot of water, including a 5-acre lake.

**The Links at Spruce Grove**—A championship course, which opened in 1983 to rave reviews. Rolling hills and water on 5 holes.

# LOS ANGELES

*"I don't want to belong to any club that would have me as a member."*
*—Groucho Marx, after being told he couldn't join a certain "restricted" club.*

The **Los Angeles Country Club** won't stand for any actors, especially famous ones, on their grounds; **Lakeside Golf Club's** members seem to be *only* famous actors. So it must be the residue of Hollywood's finest crowding up the L.A. muni courses. Whatever, pick up a reservation card at City Hall and select your tee times (for any of twelve courses) up to a week in advance, or wait it out. The pick:

**Rancho Park**—Home of the 1948 U.S. Open (won by Ben Hogan) and 1984 Los Angeles Open (when Arnold Palmer took a twelve on the eighteenth hole). Most played-on course in the world (130,000 rounds per year).

**Griffith Park Courses**—Wilson, Harding and Roosevelt (nine holes) are three scenic, undemanding courses up in the Hollywood Hills. Great landscaping and an occasional spectacular view down on the city. Fun golf (crowded, too).

# NEW YORK

In the early eighties, the American Golf Corporation purchased and rescued the city's eight courses, prying loose the death grip of the N.Y.C. Parks Department. At first, the transition was a godsend; even minimal maintenance seemed positively country-club-like to the impoverished city hackers. But modern day Big Apple wear and tear is simply too much for its golf courses to overcome—disrepair has again set in. The question remains: "Where else you gonna' play?"

Top three:

**Split Rock**—Narrow, demanding, woodsy, scenic: it's truly hard to believe this course is still in N.Y.C. (Bronx)—Big problems: poor drainage, lousy green upkeep, abandoned cars.

**Dyker Beach**—As public as it gets—Year-round play with Brooklyn views of Verrazano Bridge from every hole and occasional foghorn sound effects from passing tankers—watch out for stray dogs and nasty squatters.

**La Tourette**—N.Y.C.'s best, over rolling Staten Island terrain—Par fives kick off each nine.

# RESORTS

Every year millions of people pack up their clubs and take part in every golfer's ultimate dream: the golf vacation. *Below:* Gulfstream Golf Club in Florida is an example of the tight squeeze befalling more and more golf courses. *Opposite page:* The fifth hole at majestic Haig Point.

Not so many years ago, the idea of going somewhere on a vacation solely to play golf was comparably exotic to, say, helicopter skiing in Tibet, and just about as affordable. Sure, maybe come summer vacation time you threw some clubs in the back of the station wagon, and maybe while the rest of the crew was at the beach you got away for a round or two. But go somewhere just to think, eat, play, and sleep golf for a week? Quit dreaming.

What may have been fantasyland twenty years ago is an enjoyable reality for millions of golfers today. In fact, golf vacations, golf tours and golf resorts offer the average Joe just the kind of hotsy-totsy treatment heretofore reserved for them that's got a lot. The golf getaway makes up for playing the same local course year in and year out; it also adds that spice of course variety that is such a rewarding part of the game.

Packages of varying lengths are available at all points of the globe, and creature comforts are the premium at most spots. Here we'll deal mainly with golf facilities, rather than the availability of Jacuzzis, squash and tennis, night life, tropical drinks, etc.—but you can rest assured that the frills are available most everywhere. And with beach and/or swimming pool nearby, you might even be able to take your loved ones along on your golf holiday.

Courtesy Haig Point Golf Course/©Paul Barton

North America is nothing less than a golfer's playground. Golf courses can be found on or close to city streets, bordering cornfields, at the foot of mountains, in the middle of deserts and always, always, in and around vacation spots. For information on golfing outlets in an area you're not familiar with, consult the particular local chamber of commerce or the National Golf Foundation (telephone: (305) 744-6006). If you want to plan a vacation around golf, check the three major golf magazines *(Golf Illustrated, Golf* and *Golf Digest);* they regularly feature informative travel guides or advertising supplements that cover coast-to-coast golf. *(Golf* offers a "Vacation Planning Service" page with a mail-in for further information.) For comprehensive U.S. resort listings, see the "Golf World Resort Guide" (Golf World telephone: (404) 955-5656).

The following pages highlight seven American playlands that have recently become practically synonymous with golf: Hilton Head, South Carolina; Myrtle Beach, South Carolina; Pinehurst, North Carolina; Hawaii; Ontario, Canada; Bannif Springs, Canada; and Palm Springs, California. Of course, there are hundreds of other golf resorts from Alaska to Florida, from New Brunswick to San Diego. But these five areas have been chosen for the mere reason that each offers a lifetime of golf.

*Below:* Haig Point is a beautiful Hilton Head course, carved from raw terrain. *Right:* Harbour Town, co-designed by Jack Nicklaus and Pete Dye, is a short, but difficult, course.

# HILTON HEAD

*"There is no denying that golf has put Hilton Head on the map. After all, how many homes can you build around a tennis court?* —*Charles Price, golf writer.*

Off the very southern end of the South Carolina coastline lies Hilton Head Island, twelve by five miles long and the largest barrier reef between Long Island and the Bahamas. Always a scenic spot known for beautiful white-sand beaches, Hilton Head has over the past decade developed into a quilted topography of golf resorts and courses—over two dozen championship layouts (and counting) in 1987.

The **Sea Pines Plantation,** features three golf courses, most notably the **Harbour Town Golf Links,** co-designed by Jack Nicklaus and Pete Dye and site of the annual Heritage Classic. (Courses that appear on television as a stomping ground for professionals always score big with the hoi polloi through the rest of the year—compare-your-game-with-the-pros sort of thing, as if we didn't know how it matches up.) For championship calibre, Harbour Town is short but devious. Its relatively few traps are huge—to hit

the seventeenth green, you must avoid a surrounding eighty-yard bunker—and the narrow fairways are encroached by towering pines, palmettos and oaks. Nicklaus calls it a "thinking man's course." The **Ocean** and **Sea Marsh** courses at Sea Pines are as challenging as they are spectacular, blending salt marshes, pine woodlands and subtropical vegetation.

**Palmetto Dunes Resort** has three championship courses (along with three miles of Atlantic beach) that are characterized by a vast difference in terrain and design variety: One is intertwined with lagoons, one has yawning traps and huge, undulating greens and one is dramatically laid out over natural dunes.

**Haig Point,** on Daufuskie Island, is accessible only by ferry, just a mile across Calibogue Sound from Harbour Town. The only transportation on the 1,000-acre island is by bicycle or golf cart, the better to negotiate the masterpiece course that loops back and forth from inland hardwoods to seaside panoramas.

**Country Club of Callawassie** is surrounded by marshland and deep water rivers, yet has been designed by architect Tom Fazio to approximate the links-style courses of old Scotland, with an abundance of fairway swales, dunes and pot bunkers.

## HILTON HEAD AREA COURSES OPEN TO PUBLIC

| COURSES | HOLES/PAR | YARDAGE |
|---|---|---|
| **Country Club of Hilton Head** | | |
| Hilton Head | | |
| (803) 681-GOLF | 18/72 | 6,576 |
| **Haig Point** | | |
| Daufuskie Island | | |
| (803) 842-9293 | 18/72 | 6,746 |
| **Hilton Head Plantation** | | |
| Hilton Head | | |
| (803) 681-7717 | | |
| Dolphin Head: | 18/72 | 6,654 |
| Oyster Reef: | 18/72 | 6,934 |
| **Palmetto Dunes Resort** | | |
| Hilton Head | | |
| (800) 845-6130 | | |
| Jones: | 18/72 | 6,131 |
| Fazio: | 18/70 | 6,547 |
| Hills: | 18/72 | 6,122 |
| **Port Royal Plantation Planter's** | | |
| Hilton Head | | |
| (803) 681-3671 | | |
| Row: | 18/72 | 6,520 |
| Barony: | 18/72 | 6,530 |
| Robber's Row: | 18/72 | 6,711 |
| **Rose Hill Plantation** | | |
| Hilton Head | | |
| (803) 757-3740 | | |
| South: | 9/36 | 3,027 |
| East: | 9/36 | 3,003 |
| West: | 9/36 | 3,273 |
| **Sea Pines Plantation** | | |
| Hilton Head | | |
| (803) 671-2436 | | |
| Ocean: | 18/72 | 6,213 |
| Sea Marsh: | 18/72 | 6,086 |
| Harbour Town: | 18/71 | 5,824 |
| **Shipyard Plantation** | | |
| Hilton Head | | |
| (803) 785-2402 | | |
| Brigantine: | 9/36 | 3,352 |
| Galleon: | 9/36 | 3,364 |
| Clipper: | 9/36 | 3,466 |

The Myrtle Beach area contains over fifty golf courses in a sixty mile stretch of land. *Below:* Pine Lake, with Myrtle Beach hotels and the Atlantic Ocean in the background. *Opposite page:* The treacherous 18th at the Dunes.

# MYRTLE BEACH

The Spaniards landed on Myrtle Beach, South Carolina, in 1526, but it wasn't until 1927 that the first golf course appeared there **(Ocean Forest Golf Club,** now called **Pine Lakes).** Today there are over fifty golf courses on the sixty-mile stretch halfway between New York City and Miami that is known as the "Grand Strand." Over 10,000 golf nuts will flock to the area on any given spring day.

**Arcadian Shores,** designed by Rees Jones, whose reputation as a course architect is rapidly approaching that of his father, Robert Trent Jones, is demanding, long and tree-laden. (Many courses around Myrtle Beach have gone to some lengths to save trees and preserve natural topography—gnarled old specimens have cart paths winding around them.) **The Dunes** is part of the Pine Lakes complex; it is a most traditional course, as redesigned by Jones, Sr., with his trademark elevated greens. The clubhouse, which dates back to the twenties, is just as seclusive and reclusive, though not as exclusive, as when it was the only joint in town. **Heather Glen** was voted *Golf Digest's* best new public course in 1987, and **Oyster Bay** best new resort course in 1983.

**Myrtle Beach Golf Holiday** is a nonprofit umbrella organization that covers and links practically all of the fifty courses with all the motels, hotels, inns and resorts, for the common good of Myrtle Beach and visiting golfers. They promote all the courses and accommodate golfers of all levels (and pocketbook sizes) accordingly (telephone: (800) 845-4653).

## MYRTLE BEACH AREA COURSES OPEN TO PUBLIC

| COURSES | HOLES/PAR | YARDAGE |
|---|---|---|
| **Arcadian Shores Golf Club** | | |
| Arcadian Shores | | |
| (803) 449-5217 | 18/72 | 7,009 |
| **Azalea Sands Golf Club** | | |
| North Myrtle Beach | | |
| (803) 272-6191 | 18/72 | 6,410 |
| **Bay Tree Golf Plantation** | | |
| North Myrtle Beach | | |
| (800) 845-6191 | | |
| Gold: | 18/72 | 6,527 |
| Green: | 18/72 | 6,426 |
| Silver: | 18/72 | 6,280 |
| **Beachwood Golf Club** | | |
| North Myrtle Beach | | |
| (803) 272-6168 | 18/72 | 6,202 |
| **Burning Ridge Country Club** | | |
| Myrtle Beach | | |
| (803) 448-3141 | | |
| East: | 18/72 | 6,216 |
| West: | 18/72 | 6,237 |
| **Carolina Shores Golf Country Club** | | |
| Calabash | | |
| (803) 448-2657 | 18/72 | 6,757 |
| **Deer Track Golf Country Club** | | |
| Surfside | | |
| (803) 650-2146 | | |
| North: | 18/72 | 6,680 |
| South: | 18/72 | 6,710 |
| **Dunes Golf & Beach Club** | | |
| Myrtle Beach | | |
| (803) 449-5236 | 18/72 | 6,450 |
| **Eagle Nest Golf Club** | | |
| North Myrtle Beach | | |
| (803) 249-1449 | 18/72 | 6,900 |
| **Gator Hole Golf Course** | | |
| North Myrtle Beach | | |
| (803) 249-3543 | 18/70 | 5,600 |
| **Heather Glen Golf Links** | | |
| North Myrtle Beach | | |
| **(803) 249-9000** | **18/72** | **6,325** |
| **Heritage Plantation Golf Club** | | |
| Pawley's Island | | |
| (803) 249-3449 | 18/71 | 6,100 |
| **Indian Wells Golf Club** | | |
| Surfside Beach | | |
| (803) 651-1505 | 18/72 | 6,231 |
| **Island Green Country Club Tall** | | |
| Myrtle Beach | | |
| (803) 650-2186 | | |
| Oaks: | 9/36 | 3,017 |
| Dogwood: | 9/35 | 2,869 |
| Holly: | 9/36 | 3,035 |
| **Litchfield Golf Club** | | |
| Pawley's Island | | |
| (803) 237-3411 | 18/72 | 6,326 |

| COURSES | HOLES/PAR | YARDAGE |
|---|---|---|
| **Myrtle Beach National Golf Club** | | |
| Myrtle Beach | | |
| (803) 448-2308 | | |
| North: | 18/72 | 6,040 |
| West: | 18/72 | 6,138 |
| South: | 18/71 | 5,925 |
| **Myrtlewood Golf Course** | | |
| Myrtle Beach | | |
| (803) 449-3121 | | |
| Pines: | 18/72 | 6,068 |
| Palmetto: | 18/72 | 6,495 |
| **Oyster Bay Golf Club** | | |
| Sunset Beach | | |
| (803) 272-6399 | 18/70 | 6,800 |
| **Pine Lakes Intl. Country Club** | | |
| Myrtle Beach | | |
| (803) 449-6459 | 18/71 | 6,176 |
| **Possum Trot Golf Club** | | |
| North Myrtle Beach | | |
| (803) 272-5341 | 18/72 | 6,388 |
| **Quail Creek Golf Club** | | |
| Myrtle Beach | | |
| (803) 347-3166 | 18/72 | 6,373 |
| **Raccoon Run Golf Club** | | |
| Myrtle Beach | | |
| (803) 651-2644 | 18/71 | 6,799 |
| **River Club** | | |
| Litchfield Beach | | |
| (803) 237-8755 | 18/72 | 6,283 |
| **River Oaks Golf Plantation** | | |
| Myrtle Beach | | |
| (803) 236-2222 | 8/72 | 6,350 |
| **Robber's Roost Golf Club** | | |
| North Myrtle Beach | | |
| (803) 249-1471 | 18/72 | 6,725 |
| **Sea Gull Golf Club** | | |
| Pawley's Island | | |
| (803) 237-4285 | 18/72 | 6,295 |
| **Surf Golf Club** | | |
| Ocean Drive Beach | | |
| (803) 249-1524 | 18/72 | 6,372 |
| **Waterway Hills** | | |
| Myrtle Beach | | |
| (803) 449-6488 | | |
| Oaks: | 9/36 | 3,070 |
| Lakes: | 9/36 | 3,015 |
| Ravine: | 9/36 | 3,005 |
| **Wedgefield Plantation Country Club** | | |
| Georgetown | | |
| (803) 448-2124 | 18/72 | 6,199 |

Cut straight from the seaside pines, Myrtle Beach National offers three short, 18-hole courses.

# PINEHURST, NORTH CAROLINA

Within a fifteen-mile radius that bisects a quaint and rustic community of 3,500 lies a pine-tree paradise of over forty golf courses. In 1895, Boston scion James W. Tufts bought 5,000 acres of sand-hill timberland for a dollar an acre, with the intention of starting a springtime golf resort in the mild North Carolina climate. In 1900 he brought over Scottish professional Donald Ross to design a course: Ross wound up designing five legendary layouts at Pinehurst and another thirty-five across the state.

The **Pinehurst Country Club and Hotel** is virtually unchanged from its early days. Two monster courses have been added to bring the total to seven, which makes for the perfect golf week—a different course every day. Naturally, all courses have varying degrees of difficulty, but none, even the legendary No. 2, are prohibitively tough. What's so great about Pinehurst is the organization of the club, combined with the tradition of the place and the magnificent character of course design. In springtime, amidst flowering dogwoods, golf heaven is never far away, even if you are chipping from the pines back on to the fairway.

New courses spring up all the time in the Pinehurst area; one of the most recent and novel is **The Pit Golf Links,** spread out over an old commercial sand pit around a thirty-acre lake.

The Pit Golf Links in Pinehurst is an unusual course, laid out in the middle of a quarry.

## PINEHURST AREA COURSES OPEN TO PUBLIC

| COURSES | HOLES/PAR | YARDAGE |
|---|---|---|
| **Foxfire Resort & Country Club** | | |
| Pinehurst | 18/72 | 6,286 |
| (800) 334-9540 | 18/72 | 6,333 |
| **Hyland Hills Golf Resort** | | |
| Southern Pines | | |
| (919) 692-3752 | 18/72 | 6,024 |
| **Mid Pines** | | |
| Southern Pines | | |
| (800) 323-2114 | 18/72 | 6,515 |
| **Pinehurst Country Club** | | |
| Pinehurst | | |
| (800) 334-9553 | | |
| No. 1: | 18/70 | 5,852 |
| No. 2: | 18/72 | 6,401 |
| No. 3: | 18/71 | 5,756 |
| No. 4: | 18/72 | 6,385 |
| No. 5: | 18/72 | 6,369 |
| No. 6: | 8/72 | 6,314 |
| No. 7: | 18/72 | 6,783 |
| **Pine Needles Resort** | | |
| Southern Pines | | |
| (919) 692-7111 | 18/71 | 6,626 |
| **The Pines Golf & Resort Club** | | |
| Pinebluff | | |
| (919) 281-3165 | 18/72 | 6,605 |
| **The Pit Golf Links** | | |
| Pinehurst | | |
| (919) 944-1600 | 18/71 | 6,079 |
| **Southern Pines Country Club** | | |
| Southern Pines | | |
| (919) 692-6551 | 18/71 | 6,426 |
| **Whispering Pines Country Club & Resort** | | |
| Whispering Pines | | |
| (800) 334-9536 | | |
| No. 1 | 18/72 | 7,138 |
| No. 2 | 18/71 | 6,172 |
| No. 3 | 18/71 | 6,363 |
| **Woodlake Country Club** | | |
| Vass | | |
| (919) 245-4686 | 18/72 | 6,614 |

# ALBERTA, CANADA

In addition to having some of the most beautiful countryside in the world, Alberta boasts some of the world's most beautiful golf courses. And perhaps the most beautiful course in Alberta is the **Kananaskis Country Golf Course**—7,102 yards of Canadian Rocky Mountains, sky-blue water, and snow-topped vistas that will take your breath away. In addition, there is the famous **Banff Springs Hotel** golf course. Located in Banff National Park, it is not unusual to see a wide variety of wildlife scurrying across the course. of this Rocky Mountain resort.

## ALBERTA GOLF RESORTS

| COURSES | HOLES/PAR | YARDAGE |
|---|---|---|
| **Banff Springs Hotel**<br>Banff National Park<br>(403)762-2211 | 18/71 | 6,643 |
| **Black Bull Golf Resort**<br>Pigeon Lake<br>(403)586-2254 | 18/70 | 6,012 |
| **Edson Golf & Country Club**<br>Edson<br>(403)723-7191 | 18/71 | 6,200 |
| **Kananaskis Country Golf Course**<br>Mt. Lorette Course<br>Mt. Kidd Course<br>Canmore<br>(403)591-7070 | 18/72<br>18/72 | 7,102<br>7,049 |
| **Jasper Park Lodge Golf Course**<br>Jasper<br>(403)852-3301 | 18/71 | 6,598 |
| **River Bend Golf Course**<br>Red Deer<br>(403)343-8311 | 18/72 | 6,366 |
| **Siksika Cottage Resort**<br>Cluny<br>(403)734-3965 | 9/36 | 3,427 |
| **Wolf Creek Golf Resort**<br>Morningside<br>(403)783-6566 | 18/70 | 6,543 |

©Carl M. Purcell 1988

# HAWAII

All right, so 2,400 miles (from Los Angeles alone!) may seem like a long way to travel to play golf. But where else will a golfer find lush grass growing atop volcanic lava, ever-blooming fragrant flowers, endless beaches, spectacular sunsets—all buffered by soft trade winds? Aside from being Everyman's paradise, the fiftieth state qualifies as a bona-fide golfer's Garden of Eden. Over sixty courses beckon on the five main islands—all as lush and manicured as you'll find on the planet. If you want to go grand style, island hopping may be the ticket, while the budget-conscious may want to stay on one island. You can't really lose, either way because the courses here are beautiful.

Flanked by towering mountains, **Sheraton Makaha,** on the island of Oahu, is, as played from the championship tees, a monster. Four lakes, ninety-seven sand traps and severely undulating greens will do their best to make a hacker ignore the scenic feast. One hour from Oahu's Honolulu airport lies **Turtle Bay,** a moderately difficult flat oceanfront course (site of the Senior Skins Game) that was co-designed by Arnold Palmer and is located near some of the world's greatest surfing beaches.

On the "Garden Isle" of Kauai, the stately **Princeville** courses overlook

Hanelei Bay, where "South Pacific" was filmed. Home of the Ladie's Professional Golf Association's Kemper Open, Princeville's idyllic layout is starkly contrasted on some holes by strategically placed chunks of lava that have been known to rough up some balls. Across the island, **Wailua Municipal** is a splendid, challenging seaside course, the site of the U.S.G.A.'s Public Links Championships.

Maui, the "Valley Isle," sports seven golf resorts, the most reknowned being **Kapalua,** where the P.G.A. Tour stops twice a year. Centered amid a 23,000-acre pineapple plantation, Kapalua's two hilly, pine-lined courses (both designed by Arnold Palmer) can be quite unforgiving on breezy days, almost as unforgiving as the resort's prices ($200-$350 per day).

Hawaii, the "Big Island," offers **Mauna Kea,** the most celebrated of all the islands' courses and one of the world's most rugged oceanside courses. Mauna Kea's famous third hole juts out over a Pacific inlet and plays anywhere between 120 and 210 yards, depending on where you tee up. Robert Trent Jones redid the greens in 1975 to make them more playable for the average golfer. Nearby, on the island's west coast, is the gorgeous **Mauna Lani,** a pricey resort course cut into the black lava flow. For the traveler weary of difficult (and expensive) courses, the cross-island **Hilo Municipal** has large greens, wide fairways and no bunkers.

The snow-topped mountains at Banff Springs can cause dangerous (for your game) optical illusions. What looks like a four-iron shot, may actually be a two-wood.

# HAWAII COURSES OPEN TO PUBLIC

## OAHU

| COURSES | HOLES/ PAR | YARDAGE |
|---|---|---|
| **Alai Wai Golf Course** | | |
| Honolulu | | |
| (808) 737-2414 | 18/71 | 6,281 |
| **Hawaii Country Club** | | |
| Kunia | | |
| (808) 621-5654 | 18/72 | 5,664 |
| **Makaha Valley Country Club** | | |
| Makaha | | |
| (808) 695-9578 | 18/71 | 6,530 |
| **Mililani Golf Club** | | |
| Mililani Town | | |
| (808) 623-2254 | 18/72 | 6,369 |
| **Olomana Golf Links** | | |
| Waimanalo | | |
| (808) 259-7926 | 18/71 | 6,003 |
| **Pali Golf Course** | | |
| Pali Lookout | | |
| (808) 261-9784 | 18/72 | 6,493 |

| COURSES | HOLES/ PAR | YARDAGE |
|---|---|---|
| **Pearl Country Club** | | |
| Aiea | | |
| (808) 487-3802 | 18/72 | 6,491 |
| **Sheraton Makaha** | | |
| Makaha | | |
| (808) 695-9544 | 18/72 | 6,398 |
| **Turtle Bay Hilton & Country Club** | | |
| Kahuku | | |
| (808) 293-8811 | 18/72 | 6,400 |

## KAUAI

| COURSES | HOLES/ PAR | YARDAGE |
|---|---|---|
| **Kiahuna Golf Club** | | |
| Kauai | | |
| (808) 742-9595 | 18/72 | 6,853 |

©Doug Peebles

©Doug Peebles

**Princeville Makai Golf Club**
Hanalei
(808) 826-3580
| | | |
|---|---|---|
| No. 1 | 18/72 | 6,778 |
| No. 2 | 9/36 | 3,400 |
| No. 3 | 9/36 | 3,450 |

**Wailua Municipal Golf Course**
Lihue
(808) 245-2163        18/72       6,631

## MAUI

**Kapalua Golf Club**
Lahaina
(808) 879-3344        18/72       6,150
                            18/71       6,240

**Makena Golf Course**
Maui
(808) 879-3344        18/72       6,798

**Royal Kaanapali Golf Club**
Kaanapali Beach
(808) 661-3691
| | | |
|---|---|---|
| North: | 18/72 | 6,305 |
| South: | 18/72 | 6,250 |

**Waiehu Municipal**
Waiehu
(808) 244-5433        18/72       6,565

**Wailea Golf Club**
Wailea
(808) 877-2966

| | | |
|---|---|---|
| Orange: | 18/72 | 6,405 |
| Blue: | 18/72 | 6,300 |

## ISLAND OF HAWAII

**Hilo Municipal Golf Club**
Hilo

| | | |
|---|---|---|
| (808) 959-7711 | 18/72 | 6,584 |

**Kona Country Club**
Keauhou

| | | |
|---|---|---|
| (808) 322-3431 | 18/72 | 6,329 |
| | 9/36 | 3,082 |

**Mauna Lani**
Kohala Coast

| | | |
|---|---|---|
| (808) 885-6655 | 18/72 | 6,259 |

**Seamountain Golf Course**
Pahala

| | | |
|---|---|---|
| (808) 928-6222 | 18/72 | 6,106 |

**Volcano Golf Club**
Mauna Loa Volcano

| | | |
|---|---|---|
| (808) 967-7331 | 18/72 | 5,936 |

**Waikoloa Beach Golf Club**
Waikoloa

| | | |
|---|---|---|
| (808) 885-6060 | 18/72 | 6,645 |

**Westin Mauna Kea**
Kohala Coast

| | | |
|---|---|---|
| (800) 238-2000 | 18/72 | 6,600 |

Courtesy Deerhurst Inn & Country Club

# ONTARIO, CANADA

To most people Ontario means sparkling, fish-laden lakes, breathtaking provincial parks and game preserves, and the sprawling modern city of Toronto. To many others, Ontario means golf. Containing nearly 1000 of the country's 3000 golf courses, Ontario is the most "golfed" province in Canada. While the climate, for the most part, restricts golfing to between April and October, this recreation-minded Canadian province is the home of many fine golf courses—**Glen Abbey, Toronto Golf Club,** and **Deerhurst Golf and Country Club** to name a few. Below is a list of resorts to accommodate the most discriminating golf vacationer.

## ONTARIO GOLF RESORTS

| COURSES | HOLES/PAR | YARDAGE |
|---|---|---|
| **Bangor Lodge Golf Club**<br>Bracebridge<br>(705)645-4791 | 9/34 | 2,200 |
| **The Briars Golf and Country Club**<br>Jackson's Point<br>(416)722-3772 | 18/71 | 5,364 |
| **Deerhurst Golf and Country Club**<br>Huntsville<br>(705)789-7878 | 18/62 | 6,200 |
| **Elgin House**<br>Port Carling<br>(705)765-3101 | 9/32 | 2,395 |
| **The Homestead Golf and Country Club**<br>Durham<br>(519)369-3771 | 18/68 | 5,026 |
| **Horseshoe Valley Resort**<br>Barrie<br>(705)835-2790 | 18/72 | 6,150 |
| **Maple Hills Golf Course, at Clevelands**<br>Minett<br>(705)765-3171 | 9/32 | 1,750 |
| **Minaki Lodge Resort Golf Course**<br>Minaki<br>(807)224-4000 | 9/32 | 2,255 |
| **Oakwood Inn & Country Club**<br>Grand Bend<br>(519)238-2324 | 18/70 | 5,356 |
| **Talisman Mountain Resort**<br>Kimberley<br>(519)599-2520 | 9/31 | 2,220 |
| **Torpitt Lodge**<br>Port Stanton<br>(705)689-2633 | 9/32 | 2,100 |

*Above:* Stately Princeville overlooks Hanelei Bay, where South Pacific was filmed. *Far left:* Deerhurst Country Club, cut from a Canadian forest. *Left:* Mauni Lani, cut from the black lava.

*Below:* PGA West in La Quinta near Palm Springs. Is there a more devious course out West? *Right:* An island green on a desert course—only at PGA West.

# PALM SPRINGS

Back in the 1920s, Palm Springs was an isolated little village in the desert that offered dry, sunny climes and healing waters for the ailing, and served as a weekend retreat from nearby Los Angeles. After an oilman named O'Donnell built a nine-hole course for his friends in his front yard, a few major hotels followed suit in the early fifties. Still, the idea of golf in such an arid scene seemed farfetched. After an exploratory tour at that time of some sandy wasteland in the area, Ben Hogan told his accompanying developers, "I believe these people have all the golf they're ever going to need." How wrong he was.

**La Quinta** is the quintessential desert resort golf complex—stunning views of the Santa Rosa Mountains, lush fairways amidst stark rock settings and a demanding course design, replete with exacting fairway "landing areas." The sadistic **PGA West** not only costs $100 to play but you'll probably need to pop for a couple dozen balls to get around eighteen. Why don't you just use a bucket of range balls? **Canyon Hotel,** one of the first Palm Springs courses, has a challenging layout, framed by palm and olive trees. As is customary in most resort areas, the public may play on a daily basis at private clubs, such as the established **Indian Springs Country Club.**

Courtesy PGA West/©Brian Morgan

## PALM SPRINGS AREA COURSES OPEN TO THE PUBLIC

| COURSES | HOLES/PAR | YARDAGE |
|---|---|---|
| **Palm Springs** | | |
| (619) 323-5656 | | 6,400 |
| Desert Princess Resort | | |
| Palm Springs | | |
| (619) 322-2280 | 18/72 | 6,700 |
| **Indian Springs Country Club** | | |
| Indio | | |
| (619) 347-0651 | 18/72 | 6,260 |
| **Indian Wells Golf Resort** | | |
| Indian Wells | | |
| (619) 346-GOLF | | |
| East: | 18/72 | 6,700 |
| West: | 18/72 | 6,500 |
| **La Quinta Golf Resort** | | |
| La Quinta | | |
| (619) 345-2549 | | |
| Dunes: | 18/72 | 6,307 |
| Mountain: | 18/72 | 6,402 |
| Citrus: | 18/72 | 6,699 |
| **Marriott's Desert** | | |
| Palm Desert | | |
| (619) 341-2211 | | |
| Palms: | 18/72 | 6,381 |
| Valley: | 18/72 | 6,325 |
| **Marriott's Rancho Las Palmas** | | |
| Rancho Mirage | | |
| (619) 568-2727 | | |
| North: | 9/36 | 3,004 |
| South: | 9/35 | 3,015 |
| West: | 9/34 | 2,554 |

| COURSES | HOLES/PAR | YARDAGE |
|---|---|---|
| **Mesquite Country Club** | | |
| Palm Springs | | |
| (619) 323-1502 | 18/72 | 6,200 |
| **Mission Lakes Country Club** | | |
| Desert Hot Springs | | |
| (619) 329-6481 | 18/71 | 6,382 |
| **Mission Hills Resort Golf Club** | | |
| Rancho Mirage | | |
| (619) 328-5955 | 18/70 | 6,285 |
| **Palm Desert Country Club** | | |
| Palm Desert | | |
| (619) 345-2525 | 18/72 | 6,602 |
| **Palm Desert Resort** | | |
| Palm Desert | | |
| (619) 345-2791 | 18/72 | 6,300 |
| **Palm Springs Municipal Golf Club** | | |
| Palm Springs | | |
| (619) 328-1956 | 18/72 | 6,500 |
| **PGA West TPC** | | |
| La Quinta | | |
| (619) 564-7429 | | |
| Stadium: | 18/72 | 6,799 |
| Nicklaus: | 18/72 | 6,671 |

A beautiful flower arrangement off the fairway at Sunningdale. Looking for a lost ball in here would be frowned upon, if not grounds for expulsion.

# ENGLAND, SCOTLAND AND IRELAND

*"In Britain, you skip the ball, hop it, bump it, run it, hit under it, on top of it, and then hope for the right bounce."* —Doug Sanders, Sports Illustrated, *1984.*

Perhaps you've heard that the ancestral game as played in the British Isles is markedly different than that played in the United States. This is usually true, largely due to their idea of how the grounds should (or shouldn't) be groomed. The rough is, at the very least, by definition just that, the fairways often don't begin until 150 yards out from the tee, and the greens can be as hard and slick as Carrara marble. In addition, gusty winds on seaside courses can remove any semblance of leisure from the golfing experience. But for any serious golfer with a sense of the game's history, there is no equal to the thrill and challenge of playing *over there.*

©Brian Morgan

The nicest thing about overseas golf in general is that it's so uncomplicated. True, you need a letter of introduction from your club (hey, borrow some stationery—even public courses have letterheads) to play some of the tonier clubs, but by and large all courses are available to the traveler, especially on weekdays (weekends are often reserved for members only), at very reasonable rates. Just don't call at the last minute, or, worse yet, show up unannounced at the clubhouse.

There are more than 2100 courses spread out over the United Kingdom (England, Ireland, Scotland, Wales). Most are distinguished by a Spartan lack of frills, military adherence to rules, superb maintenance, speedy play (any foursome taking over four hours to play eighteen risks ostracism from fellow-members), and the total nonexistence of golf cars, though handcarts are allowed. Caddies are nearly always available, if you can bear the scrutiny. The idea is that the game should be rugged yet enjoyable—a contradiction in terms, perhaps? Not for mad dogs and Englishmen.

## PICK OF THE BEST

Picking the five "best" courses in the land where the game began is certainly arbitrary, if not downright imperious. Well, what we're trying to do here is to offer a cross-section of the best of U.K. golf. For sure there won't be a better fifteen courses around, although there may be several hundred not far behind. Bear in mind that the fabled St. Andrews, Muirfield, Ballybunion and Royal County Down courses have been omitted from this section, since they appear earlier in "Best" (see p.94).

# ENGLAND

## Sunningdale, Surrey

Sunningdale, fifty to sixty miles southwest of London, is one of the many fine inland "heathland" courses that cropped up in the area near the turn of the century. Designed in 1900 by two-time Open champion Willie Park, Jr., Sunningdale was revolutionary in construction, because, for the first time, tees and greens were built up above fairway level. Fairway "landing areas" were also elevated, and bold, man-made hazards, were added as well.

The club is elegant and reeks with history. Its captains include the Prince of Wales and the Duke of York, and it was here that Bobby Jones, qualifying for the 1927 British Open, shot a sixty-six that still stands as one of the finest, steadiest rounds of championship golf ever played.

## Walton Heath, Surrey

Literally dug from an undergrowth of heather, rhododendrons and Scotch fir, Walton Heath (old course) opened to a horde of dignitaries in 1904. Like nearby Sunningdale, Walton Heath was a pioneering effort in shaping and contouring the land. Its architect, W. Herbert Fowler, rode horseback through the gorse for two years, planning proper green sites and tracking the holes. Fowler was also one of the first to strategically plant trees about a golf course. Today, there are two courses to choose from (6,813 yards, 6,659 yards); the most difficult holes from both are used for tournaments.

Walton Heath's rough-side heather blooms pale yellow in the spring and lavender in the fall, but such eye-pleasers had best be viewed from the fairways. Hitting out of the scrubby stuff can wring your hands like a spin cycle and do no better for your score.

## TWO TOP TOURING GUIDES

For those golfers headed for ye olde sod on their own—that is, without some sort of package-tour setup—two books are highly recommended. A.A.'s (an English auto service) "Guide to Golf Courses in England" (Salem House, $21.95) is available in large bookstores and many pro shops and golf outlets. It is an invaluable Michelin-style guide to traveling and playing golf in England, Wales and Scotland. Information is given on how to reach each course, whether or not an introduction is required, what facilities (lodging and food) are available and what type of course to expect. Symbols clarify everything from bar hours to green fees.

*The Benson and Hedge's Golfer's Handbook* (Macmillan, London) is an annual publication full of facts and trivia, most notably a fairly complete listing of golf courses in the U.K., along with a compendium of hotels and inns. In the Handbook a traveler can find a club's phone number, the name of the club secretary (this is very important; when in doubt as to how to proceed, you can ring up for a gentlemanly and humble inquiry, which sometimes will work), greens fees and visitors policy. You can even look up the course record, if it proves to your interest.

©Brian Morgan

## Royal Lytham and St. Anne's, Lancashire

Just up the Irish Sea coastline from Birkdale lies St. Anne's, an equally awesome links course and host to nine British Opens, most recently in 1988. Seve Ballesteros won it in 1979 with the famous shot from the parking lot, but he credits his bunker play more than anything else for the victory. There are over 200 sand traps on this course, many of them lurking on the edge of narrow fairways. With the widely varying directions of holes, the wind, at least, is fair, but don't be misled by an opening par-three hole. The par-seventy-one course is a hearty 6,822 yards long, and with all the traps, it can easily offer the errant striker a day at the beach.

## Royal Birkdale, Lancashire

*"At fifteen, we put down my bag to hunt for a ball—found the ball, lost the bag."*
—*Lee Trevino,* Sports Illustrated, *1983.*

Birkdale is just near enough to the Irish Sea to invite a perpetually howling wind down into its winding-valley fairways. Craggy sand hills crawling with gorse and willow scrub will swallow anything off-line. Buried in the stuff at the sixteenth, Arnold Palmer carved a 6-iron to within ten feet of the pin for a birdie that won the 1961 British Open (a nearby plaque commemorates the feat). This is a grand and desolate course—bleak, in the classic tradition of "Wuthering Heights," and over 7,000 yards long. For those who might not yet be mentally and physically exhausted after sixteen holes, the course finishes with two long par fives. Royal Birkdale is top-notch British Open terrain, championship stuff—inspiring for eighties-or-lower shooters, but a possible golf hell for the rest.

# Royal St. George, Kent

*"You're like a blind man with a pretty girl—you have to feel your way around."*
—*Golf pro Peter Jacobsen on St. George.*

Why do we keep talking about sand? Because the Brits have such a fondness for the stuff on their golf courses. If you hit nice long drives that always landed in the fairway, the game might be boring—supposedly. At the par-three third at Royal St. George, any shot not reaching the green will probably find sand along the way. The hole is aptly called Sahara. Any wonder the best British player's name is Sandy?

Actually, hitting long, straight drives at Royal St. George, commonly known as "Sandwich" (for the name of the town it lies in, not for the course topography), may help one avoid the many bunkers (called "corsets") that pinch the fairways. Sandy Lyle did just that to win the Open in 1985. Only an hour due east of London by train, Sandwich is of the same class as the Channel Coast courses. Jack Nicklaus won the St. George Challenge Cup in 1959 with a 149 (two rounds)—nine over par—which members at the time considered a stellar performance.

Cushy and comfortable, the clubhouse at Sandwich is an exception to the rule in England. Best enjoy it, for the golf course is anything but.

©Brian Morgan

*Below:* Royal Dornoch, one of the best-kept secrets among the world's greatest courses. *Right:* Royal Troon, where the back nine plays mostly into the wind. *Opposite page:* Gleneagles, a beautiful inland course in the moors, where streams and dells abound.

# SCOTLAND

## Carnoustie

*"A good swamp spoiled."* —*Gary Player,* Golf World, *1975.*

Situated a half hour north of Dundee along the Firth of Tay, Carnoustie seems to perpetually sit under stark, gray skies that do, on occasion, open up. The course was conceived by the first real "course designer"—renowned ballmaker Allan Robertson, who laid out ten holes worth of links in 1844. It was later repeatedly remodeled by some of the great names of British golf: Willie Park, Jr., Old Tom Morris, and, lastly, James Braid, who left it with "championship" status and length (7,065 yards) in 1926.

Carnoustie is public—reservations are needed during peak season—and serviced by a cadre of caddies who sport coat and tie (and often overcoats) in just about any season. Ben Hogan won here in 1953, in his only entry in a British Open.

## Royal Dornoch

Royal Dornoch, where golf was played as early as 1616 (the present layout dates back, to World War II), is the quaintest, most out-of-the-way grand championship course to be found in the world today. Perhaps that's why it doesn't draw the attention given to the other "great" links. But among golf cognoscenti and course architects this course has few equals anywhere.

The links of Dornoch are located fifty miles north of Inverness, on Scottish highlands overlooking the North Sea. Perhaps unimpressive at first, the course, after a few holes, opens to ravishing golf country. The look is one of antiquity, a place untouched for centuries. The contours are soft and billowy; the fairway turf is close-cropped, full, and firm; and the rough, for once, is actually playable, with an absence of the *scrag* and *gorse* that characterizes so many Scottish links. The mesa-like greens rest atop severe inclines, placing a premium on finesse chipping. It was here that master architect Donald Ross grew up; Royal Dornoch's transatlantic imprint is cast on over 600 courses that he designed in the United States.

©Brian Morgan

©Brian Seed

©Brian Seed

# Gleneagles

There is inland golf in Scotland, and quite stunning at that. The grand Gleneagles Hotel has four courses that blend into an idyllic Scottish countryside. The King's course is the most wellknown and difficult, yet its severity is tempered by a scenic moorland topography replete with pines and streams. Ironically, the courses here all sport the English "heathland" design influence—especially the King's and Queen's courses, laid out by James Braid in 1919. Morning and early-afternoon play is reserved to hotel guests, but where else could a traveler possibly want to stay but in such classic digs?

# Royal Troon

Troon's devilish 126-yard, par-three eighth hole, the "postage stamp," was the site of some famous holes in one over the years that the British Open was held there. Gene Sarazen, well past retirement age, had one in 1973, fifty years after his first Open. With the usually prevailing tail winds, this hole's green is about as easy to land on as the hood of a Volkswagen. In addition, the hole belies Troon's testing total length, which stretches to 7,065 yards. The long back nine, usually played into the wind, is particularly trying. Because of these extremes, and because it borders on an international airport's runway, Troon will always be a controversial Open site.

*Below:* Rugged Turnberry, host to some recent historic British Opens, was reconverted from an airstrip in 1951. *Opposite page:* County Sligo in Yeats country.

# Turnberry

After seeing Turnberry bring the world's greatest golfers to their knees at the 1986 British Open, many visitors are pleasantly shocked by the course's playability. Well, for one thing the wind doesn't always howl up to fifty miles per hour as it did then, and fairways at championships are narrowed, while the rough is allowed to grow. (Greg Norman's ability to accurately bore a 1-iron through the wind off the tees won him the Championship.)

For oceanside links, Turnberry most resembles Pebble Beach (see "Best" p 94), with the fifth through tenth holes skirting the coastline. The course dates back to 1903, but was converted to an airstrip during World War II and then redesigned in 1951. Under pluperfect conditions in 1977, Tom Watson battled Jack Nicklaus stroke for stroke over four days to win by one shot with a record-breaking 268. To one side of the course, the mammoth Turnberry Hotel is a reminder of the awaiting hospitality; to the other, the Ailsa Craig, an enormous rock island, is a dark and foreboding witness to the elements.

©Brian Seed

©Brian Seed

# IRELAND

## County Sligo

The first four holes at County Sligo inauspiciously introduce the course: uphill, protected and inland. From the fifth it becomes the prototypical links: a 100-foot drop to a group of fairways surrounded by beach and bays. The strangest hole on the course is the fourteenth, a double-dogleg par four that invariably plays into the wind. Across the water, looms Ben Bulben, Yeats' fabled flat-topped mountain. Yeats, now buried in a nearby cemetery, wrote his own epitaph in "Under Ben Bulben":

    . . . On limestone quarried near the spot
  By his command these words are cut:
  Cast a cold eye
  On life, on death.
  Horseman, pass by!

Raised tees offer spectacular countryside views at Lahinch, a short but rugged course. Laid out in 1893 by "old" Tom Morris, this sentimental favorite is known as the St. Andrews of Ireland.

# Lahinch, *County Clare*

Lahinch is a short course by championship standards (6,276 yards) and a sentimental Irish favorite. Known as the St. Andrews of Ireland, the course was, in fact, laid out in 1893 by "old" Tom Morris, the St. Andrews pro. Length aside, the course is rugged and intriguing in a sometimes amusing fashion, as with the "Dell," the famous 156-yard sixth hole. The green, surrounded by sand hills, lies in a valley, invisible from the tee, but a painted rock that faces the tee points the way, depending on daily pin placement. The lofty tees afford phenomenal views of the countryside.

# Portmarnock, *County Dublin*

Portmarnock is the longest and probably the most difficult course in the British Isles. Arnold Palmer has called it the greatest course in the world, which is certainly open to more debate than if he had said "toughest." It certainly is grand and sweeping, and has the type of layout that makes you study each hole. The course winds around in a figure eight, allowing the golfer some wind respite. The swooping fairway hills are bordered by sand dunes and sea marsh, but the Irish are said never to lose balls.

# Royal Dublin

The oldest golf club in Ireland, Royal Dublin actually lies within city limits. The course is somewhat more forgiving than nearby Portmarnock in that it's 600 yards shorter. Its narrow fairways, however, will quickly humble the hackers. From the tee at the par-four fifth, Danny Kaye's caddie asked him what he needed. Looking down at a needle-threader, ringed with tall rough and a green 428 yards away, he answered, "A rifle."

# Waterville, *County Kerry*

Waterville is a terribly long, "modern" course, built half on links, half on rolling moors. Fortunately, it plays downhill, with a plentitude of varying tee areas. The course was the 1972 brainchild of John Mulcahy, an American industrialist and Nixon campaign contributor, but we won't hold that against it. The seventeenth tee is 100 feet high, but no hole is as unpredictable as the 587 yard eighteenth. Facing a strong headwind, the resident pro once needed two drivers and a 1-iron to reach the green. The next day, playing with a tail wind, he used a driver and a 9-iron to land six feet from the pin.

## TOUR PACKAGES

For the well-heeled and less adventurous, there are many golfing package tours available to the UK—to all over the world, for that matter. Any travel agent will have some brochures. **University Golf Overseas** (telephone: (617) 797-3030) offers low prices on trips to England based on organizing two foursomes and provides a station wagon per foursome, as well as tee times at the courses of choice. They also offer Ireland, Scotland or a combination of both, and a special price for an extra week, for golf junkies who can't yet face the return trip home. **Royal Viking Line** offers lap-of-luxury ocean-liner golf cruises worldwide (South Pacific, Panama Canal, Southeast Asia)—their best bet is the British Isles cruise, with Gary Player as adviser. **Intergolf** (telephone: 800-363-6273) has tours of great Scottish and Irish courses for anywhere from four to eighteen days, either "independent" or "escorted." They also offer extended French Riviera, Morocco/Spain, Portugal and Bermuda tours.

# OFF-THE-BEATEN-PATH GOLF

Due to the obsessive nature of those who play it, golf has become an irrepressible pastime; that's why courses can be found in the strangest places, on some of the farthest reaches of the planet. A Chicagoan named Patrick O'Bryan recognized this and organized a madcap tour of the strangest spots on the globe to play golf (highest, southernmost, etc.) in 1986. Astronaut Alan Shepard fueled the fire when he moon-struck his 6-iron back in 1969. Ike was always putting in the White House, and Walter Hagen hit golf balls off his ocean liner and off the roof of the Savoy in London.

## KUWAIT

The greens are actually "browns" at the **Hunting and Equestrian Club** in Kuwait, oiled down with petroleum so that the steamrolled sand won't blow away. The fairways and the rough are both sand; one can be distinguished from the other by markers and by the rule that a golfer may place a patch of artificial grass under his ball in the "fairway" but not in the "rough." The trick is to keep the swatch—every golfer carries one clipped to his bag—from sliding all over the place. The temperature usually hovers around 100 degrees on the course, the first ten holes of which are the infield of a racetrack; golf isn't played on Monday, when the horses race. There is no actual hunting either—the only animals on the course are lizards.

## HIGHEST, COLDEST

The highest golf course in the world is thought to be the **Tuctu Golf Club** in Peru, at 14,335 feet above sea level. The **La Paz Golf Club,** in Bolivia, reaches 13,550 feet. The most scenic mountain course is **Crans,** in Switzerland, with a majestic layout that overlooks the Alps.

Coldest-course honors must go to the **High Country Club,** 400 miles inside the Arctic Circle, on the shores of the Beaufort Sea in Northern Canada. The nine-hole course with sand greens was founded in 1975 by missionary Dave Freeman and boasts a membership of 700.

## PRISON GOLF

Private golf lessons in England cost from $15 to $20 an hour, unless one is lucky enough to become a prisoner at one of the country's top-security jails. That's right, jailhouse golf. At the Coldingley Jail, inmates receive tips on the soccer field from golf professional Arthur Roe, who brings no club bigger than a 6-iron, so that the shots won't clear the prison's forty-foot wall. Prison staff members don't qualify for lessons and are considerably miffed, but the prison administration says the outdoors is good for the men.

A sand green on a course in Saudia Arabia; the surface is oiled for protection from the wind.

# AIRPORT GOLF

The game is tough enough; imagine having to worry about the planes. At Laurens, Iowa, the local airport doubles as a golf club. The lone grass runway occupies part of seven of the course's first nine holes. Golfers are told to look both ways and up before swinging, but there seems to be a mutual respect between fliers and golfers. Pilots will circle and buzz once before landing, at which time the golfers move aside. Planes have the right of way.

# CHINA

Chairman Mao's Cultural Revolution may have had other goals, but after an absence of fifty years, golf has returned to mainland China. **Zhongshan Hot Springs,** designed by Arnold Palmer, is a glorious course that offers spectacular views of fourteenth-century Ming Dynasty tombs and of water buffalo pulling wooden plows through the adjoining rice paddies. The greens are immaculately hand-sprinkled, the fairways are watered by underground irrigation. Temperatures throughout the year approximate southern Florida, except during the typhoon season of August-October, when gales can reach 125 miles per hour.

# THIRD-WORLD GOLF

Frank Cox was a newspaper executive who played over 1500 courses worldwide before he died in 1982. Some of the more unusual courses he played:

**Panmunjom,** in Korea (on the 38th Parallel, had a four-tee green bordering on a mine field). At **Moose Run,** in Anchorage, Alaska, moose and bear were both attractions and hazards. The **Mena House Golf Club,** in Cairo, was overrun by hawkers selling everything from soda and fruit to golf lessons. **Royal Nepal** was grandly surrounded by Himalayas but wound its way through native huts and grazing cattle oblivious to the golf. Cox, who once hit a ball off the Great Wall of China, must have had great concentration.

# IRON CURTAIN GOLF

A pleasant surprise for Western travelers is the existence of golf courses in Eastern Europe. While the scene is not quite as together as, say, golf in Scotland, there is no small charm in banging the ball around the Danube.

**Kek Duna** (Blue Danube) is Hungary's only course. There are only six holes, with possibly the world's toughest 48-yard par three—sand in front of the green, low-hanging tree branches over it. **Bled,** in Yugoslavia, is a gorgeous, hilly course at the base of the Julian Alps. It is a top-shelf resort, with a bucolic tenth-century castle that leans out over a crystal-clear mountain lake.

Czechoslovakia's **Marianske Lazne** is the old Marienbad spa, and the site of a lush golf course originally laid out for England's King Edward VII, who used to spend summers there.

Mena House in Egypt. Can you beat a pyramid for a backdrop?

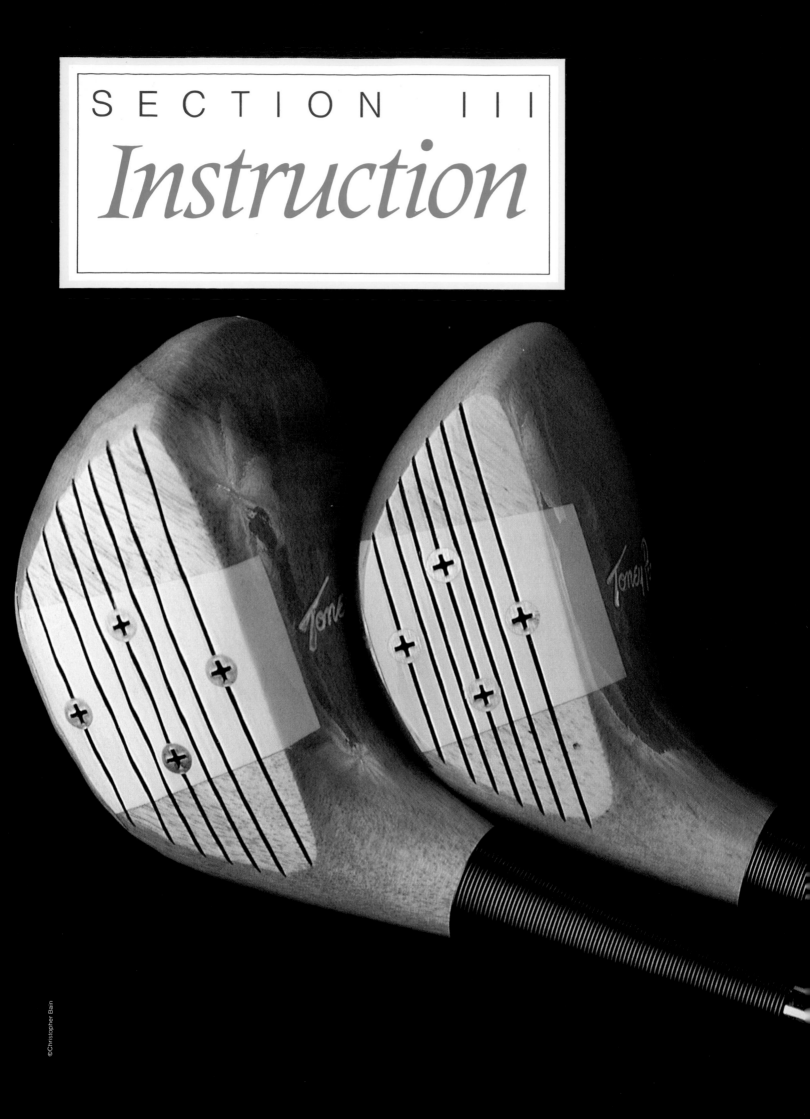

# SECTION III

## *Instruction*

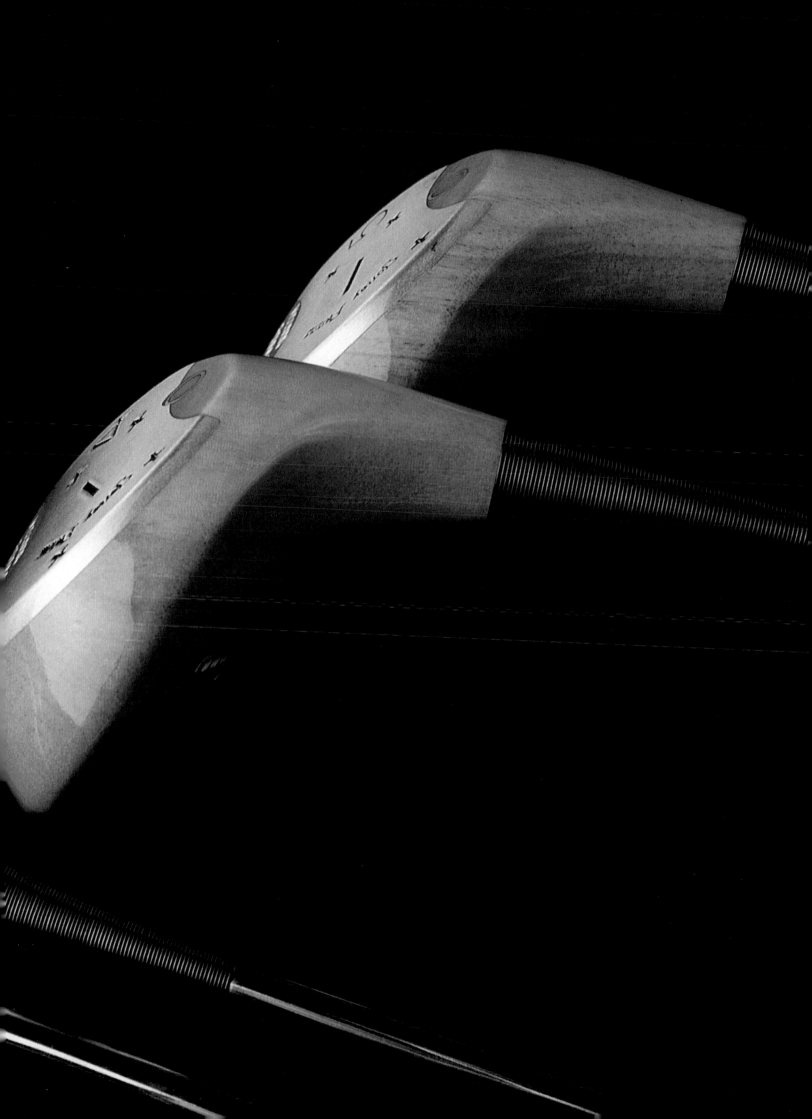

Head down, eyes on the ball, rotate the hips, rock those feet, elbows in, don't overgrip, relax the forearms, don't lock the wrists, follow through—is there any end to the list of things to remember while trying to hit the damn ball? Not really. Just when you thought it was safe to swing freely, you've found out—or someone has found out for you—that some seemingly minute element of your game is out of whack, and the duck hook is back. You correct it—something about the grip being too "strong," too "right-hand oriented"—and before you know it you're pushing the ball to the right. The inherent frustration in golf never ends, on any level. Just watch most professional golfers after they've hit a shot, any shot—they're rarely satisfied, often downright disgusted. But the payback is that there's also no limit to improvement, no limit to personal satisfaction when improvement does occur.

Because there has always been this need to improve that festers in the heart and soul of each and every golfer, thousands of books have been written on the game. Of late, hundreds of home videos have joined golf's instructional miasma. Add the schools, computer-swing analyzers, private instructors, clinics, training methods and even personal gurus, and you all but need a course on how to find out what type of instruction might be good for you. Here's a sampler of some of the best and most famous books, videos, schools and gadgets.

# BOOKS

The first book ever written on golf appeared in Scotland in 1743: *The Goff, An Heroic-Comical Poem in Three Cantos,* by Thomas Mathison. Only twenty-four pages long, *The Goff* was later reprinted in 1763 and 1793, costing four pence at the time. At auction, a first edition recently fetched $15,000, but reprints can be had for as little as $40.

It's doubtful that Bob Hope's *Confessions of a Hooker,* Tom Watson's *The New Rules of Golf,* or Jack Nicklaus' *Golf My Way* will ever bring more than jacket price—they're only mentioned here as three random, albeit successful, titles among the hundreds of golf books, mostly instructional, published yearly over the past decade. Many golf tomes invariably find their way to the remainder piles in used-book stores, but no matter—golf remains far and away the most written about of all sports. The U.S.G.A.'s library at Golf House, in Far Hills, New Jersey, holds over 7,000 volumes; there's even a sourcebook out that's solely geared to locating other golf books.

The following survey capsulizes some of the most famous and respected instructional golf books of the past century. Afterward, there appears a varied selection of mostly recent golf writings of all sorts.

# THE ART OF GOLF

Sir Walter Simpson (Edinburgh, 1887)

*"Unlike the other Scotch game of whisky-drinking, excess in it is not injurious to the health."*

One of the early masters of golf writing, Simpson combined instructional savvy—he was the first to use photographs—with psychological insight: "All those who drive thirty yards suppose themselves to be great putters." All great golf writers have paid literary homage to Simpson, despite his rather radical teaching concept that accepted varying swing styles for different players. His literary style, however, set the table for the evolution of the very highest form of sportswriting.

# PLAY GREAT GOLF

by Arnold Palmer (Doubleday, 1987)

In the same vein as Tommy Armour's book, though on a much grander scale, Palmer keeps the instruction uncomplicated and basic by focusing on five key fundamentals: grip, address, takeaway, head position and acceleration (these are his five fundamentals, anyway). Drawings and photos throughout and sections on "thinking game," "putting" and "trouble shots" complement the book. This last should be a book in itself for all the hackers who spend their golf days in the traps, rough and woods.

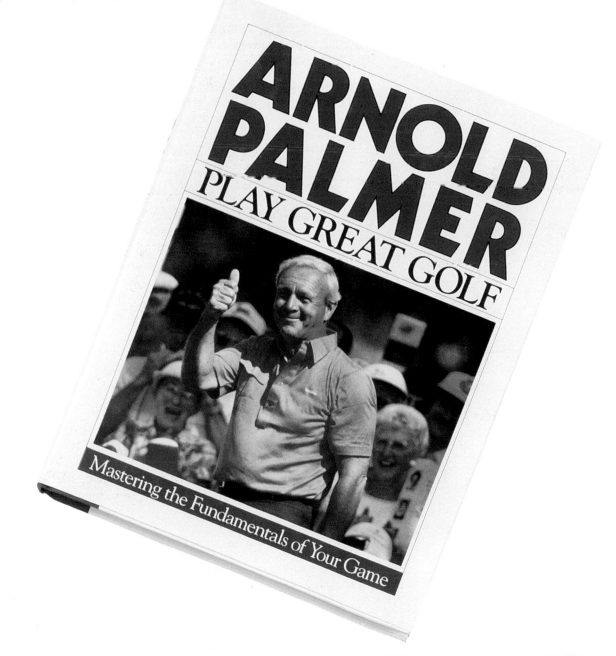

# DOWN THE FAIRWAY

Bobby Jones and O.B. Keeler (Minton, Balch & Co., 1927)

The collaboration of golf's most articulate player and one of its most erudite writers left behind this classic narrative text about the genteel, competitive life of championship golf in the twenties. Jones was only twenty-five when he co-wrote the book, yet his observations on life and golf belied his age. Always respectful to the reader, always humble in relating his own experiences, Bobby Jones taught in the same way he played the game: with dignity, control and precision.

# A NEW WAY TO BETTER GOLF

Alex Morrison (Simon & Schuster, 1932)

Morrison was a cantankerous Los Angeleno who devoted a lifetime to studying the golf swing, the better to teach celebrity pupils such as Babe Ruth, Henry Ford and Douglas Fairbanks. He expounded that the swing is a function of the body's left side, through which all force should be generated. He was also a proponent of pointing the chin behind the ball, rolling the feet and the interlocking grip, all of which typify the style of Jack Nicklaus, whose mentor was Jack Grout, a Morrison assistant. Morrison divides the golf swing into eight stages, bringing a detailed anatomical bearing to each.

# ON LEARNING GOLF

Percy Boomer (Knopf, 1946)

Percy Boomer was a legendary British teacher who believed in reproducing the "feel" of correct action, which he labeled "muscle memory," a term widely used today. He theorized that the golf swing was but a series of connected sensations that the muscles could, through repetition, routinely learn to reproduce. His most famous image was that of "turning in a barrel." By this he meant visualizing swinging within a hip-high barrel, big enough to allow a golfer's hips to turn and rotate properly, yet narrow enough to restrict lateral movement.

# HOW TO PLAY
# YOUR BEST GOLF ALL THE TIME

Tommy Armour (Simon and Schuster, 1953)

*"Action before thought is the ruination of most of your shots."*

Tommy Armour was one of the few golf greats whose reputation as a teacher equaled his record as a competitor. (He won the U.S. Open, P.G.A., and British Open in the same year.) As a teaching manual, his book is one of the most lucid, simple and concise treatises ever written on the game. It's strength is an intentional absence of detail—all to keep the pupil from becoming confused. Armour sets forth the basic fundamentals and elements of good golf, with the help of a fine set of illustrations by Leland Gustavson. Throughout, Armour stresses what to do, not what not to do. His most radical precept advises "whacking the hell out of the ball with the right hand."

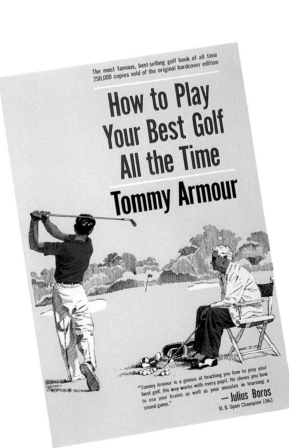

The most famous, best-selling golf book of all time
250,000 copies sold of the original hardcover edition

How to Play Your Best Golf All the Time
Tommy Armour

"Tommy Armour is a genius at teaching you how to play your best golf. His way works with every pupil. He shows you how to use your brains as well as your muscles in learning a sound game."
— Julius Boros
U. S. Open Champion 1963

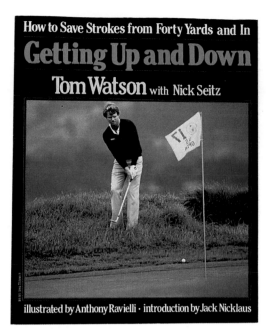

# THE COMPLETE GOLFER

Harry Vardon (McLure, Phillips, 1905)

Britain's great turn-of-the-century golfer Harry Vardon is most revered and remembered for two legacies: the fluid golf swing and the overlapping grip. Pre-Vardon swings were upright, closed, and restrained, until his grace, rhythm, and style became a standard that to this day has barely changed. *The Complete Golfer* was the first popular instruction book and has been reprinted over twenty times. The book painstakingly details all the elements of the Vardon method, at the same time uniting all golfers against the adversities, with such typical subheadings as "The Mistakes of a Beginner," "Despair That Follows," and "All Men May Excel."

# GETTING UP AND DOWN

Tom Watson (Vintage, 1983)

One of the best texts ever on the short game, Watson's book economically delineates the proper putting stroke, chipping and pitching and sand play. From forty yards in no one plays the game better than Watson, and here he provides the basic principles to mastering the delicate art of "getting up and down"—from the forty-yard bunker shot to the three-foot putt. For developing these skills, he also presents many entertaining practice drills. A most lucid presentation—now all we have to do is execute.

# THE NINE BAD SHOTS OF GOLF (AND WHAT TO DO ABOUT THEM)

Jim Dante and Leo Diegel, with Len Elliott (Whittlesey House, 1947)

Some duffers would argue that there has to be more than nine bad shots, but this concept made for a huge seller in its first decade of print. The shots:

Slicing: Hitting with an open face.
Hooking: Hitting with a shut face.
Topping: Hitting with a lifted head.
Smothering: Hitting with a hooded club face.
Pulling: Hitting from outside in.
Pushing: Hitting inside out.
Skying: Hitting with chopping downswing.
Sclaffing: Hitting with too much weight on right foot.
Shanking: Hitting with no pivot.

## FIVE LESSONS

by Ben Hogan and Herbert Warren Wind (Fireside, 1957)

Originally appearing as five articles in *Sports Illustrated,* Hogan and Wind's co-efforts have resulted in the clearest possible testament to the technical side of golf greatness. The book is one of the most influential ever written on golf. The lessons are: Grip, Stance, Swing (parts 1 and 2), and Summary. Most fascinating are Hogan's "swing plane" principles, in which the arms should stay parallel to an imaginary diagonal pane of glass. Thanks to Tony Ravielli's anatomically instructive illustrations, the power of Hogan's swing positively vibrates off the pages.

## THE SEARCH FOR THE PERFECT GOLF SWING

Alastair Cochran and John Stobbs (J.B. Lippincott, 1968)

*Search* is primarily a scientific study, but one that answers most of golf's fundamental questions, from driver to putter—what actually happens from the beginning of the swing off the tee to when the ball rolls in the cup. The team of British scientists, commissioned by The Golf Society of Great Britain, used equipment such as a force-analysis platform (to study stress between a golfer's feet and the ground) and a wind tunnel (to gauge ball aerodynamics). The captivating scientific artwork superimposes colored designs over black-and-white demonstration photos. A great text for the analytically minded golf student.

## THE SQUARE-TO-SQUARE GOLF SWING

Dick Aultman (Golf Digest, 1970)

This method was all the rage when it first came out, and some golfers still swear by it (or at it). Square-to-square was actually first represented in H. G. Whigham's 1897 text *How To Play Golf.* The principal idea is to line up squarely behind the ball and square to the target line. Aultman promotes a continuous straight-line relationship that will hopefully produce a square club head at impact and result in accuracy. Note that the system is based on a "dominant" left side, diametrically opposed to Bobby Jones and Tommy Armour's "right-side-club-whipping" recommendations.

# GOLF BEGINS AT FORTY

Sam Snead (Dial, 1978)

With a swing that hasn't lost much over sixty years, Sam Snead plays a unique brand of "old man's golf." What he tries to impart in his book is that it's never too late to start developing smart swing habits, and that every golfer over forty need not swing like a rusty gate. Solutions lie variously in getting more from your body, having a more "mature" outlook toward club selection, putting with the arms, and "pulling the trigger" sooner. Snead also has an unintentionally funny "turning pounds into yards" section for overweight golfers, enabling them to get out of the way of their own backswings.

# THE INNER GAME OF GOLF

Tim Gallwey (Random House, 1979)

Much like Gallwey's phenomenally successful *Inner Game of Tennis*, this book is deep and heady stuff. The self-image barrier, the "expectations" game and fear of failure are just a few of the psychological topics covered in this exploration of the golfing id. There are no gimmicks and tips in the book, just some subtle ideas on trusting the body and relaxed concentration. A typical passage wrestles with the Zen problem of caring too much or too little and finding the balance between the two extremes. Did anyone say golf was a mental game?

# PLAY BETTER GOLF, Vols. I & II

Jack Nicklaus (Pocket Books, 1980, 1981)

Far less famous than his classic best-seller *Golf My Way,* these two paperbacks are actually more entertaining, especially when you realize they come from one of the more no-nonsense athletes of all time. Here Nicklaus teaches via a comic-book format. The reading is light, and the first volume is divided into ten basics tenets (e.g., "swing the same with every club," "strive for a full arc," "wind your spring"). Volume II deals with the short game, offering such tips as "play safe from the sand," "be firm on short uphillers," and "make the hole look like a bucket" (this last takes no small imagination).

Ben Hogan

with
Herbert Warren Wind
and drawings by
Anthony Ravielli

Five Lessons
The Modern Fundamentals of Golf

# *MISCELLANEOUS GOLF BOOKS*

## GOLF IN THE KINGDOM

Michael Murphy (Delta, 1971)

Based on the author's golf pilgrimage to Scotland, the book is a semi-autobiographical account of meeting a golf guru (Shivas Irons) at an age-old Scottish links. From that point on, the narrator's entire approach to the game—and, of course, life—changes dramatically toward the awestruck. Could change the way you view the game, too, depending on how susceptible you are to consciousness-raising and enlightenment.

## FOLLOWING THROUGH

Herbert Warren Wind (Ticknor & Fields, 1985)

Twenty years of golf writing as seen through the eyes of a master make up this sterling collection of articles. Their subjects vary from the young and pudgy Jack Nicklaus to Bing Crosby, from out-of-the-way Scottish courses to the sacred tradition of the Masters. Wind, the latest in the long line of fine golf writers, balances his reverence with great technical knowledge.

## STROKES OF GENIUS

Thomas Boswell (Doubleday, 1986)

Again a compilation of stories, this time from the pages of the *Washington Post* and *Golf Magazine*. Boswell's chronicles of the golf tour (Nicklaus's 1986 Masters win, architect Pete Dye's "stadium" courses) and the modern-day pro (Craig Stadler, Fuzzy Zoeller) are top shelf, highlighted by evocative Richard Darcey photos.

## PIGEONS, MARKS, HUSTLERS

Sam Snead with Jerry Tarde (Golf Digest, 1986)

*"I've always believed in playing golf for a little something, even if it's just fifty cents a side."*

When not playing tournament golf, Sam Snead has spent his life playing twenty-dollar Nassaus (and often much higher), negotiating bets, and dodging hustlers. This book is a maverick's sharing of a lifetime's worth of shrewd golf knowledge, a wealth of wagering wisdom around the clubhouse. In his endearing country-shark fashion, Snead tells how to: spot a hustler, press the bet, deal with cheaters, collect a bet, read your opponents and more—a must for the weekend gambler.

# SNAKE IN THE SAND TRAP

Lee Trevino with Sam Blair (Henry Holt, 1985)

*"A good driver is a helluva lot harder to find than a good wife."*

Trevino's early golf days and tour memoirs will appeal to all blue-collar golfers and everyday fans. In this pithy anecdotal collection, the Tex-Mex gabber reminisces on everything from golf hustlers to royalty. Here's one golfer who's had a good time on his way to the top.

# TEED OFF

Dave Hill with Nick Seitz (Prentice Hall, 1977)

Characteristically brash and outspoken, *Teed Off* is a collection of diatribes against the P.G.A. tour from golf's all-time bad boy. In a candid, colorful fashion, pro Dave Hill takes off on a multitude of controversies: cheating, slow play, pill taking and drab players among them.

# THE GREEN ROAD HOME

Michael Bamberger (Contemporary, 1986)

Michael Bamberger's insightful collection of tour tales is the result of a year's caddying on the pro tour. The modern caddie's importance on the tour is commonly ignored, an oversight the author handily corrects. Impressions of champions and hangers-on abound, but most captivating are his takes on fellow-caddies, such as the crusty Lee Lynch, a man who's hauled bags for seven decades.

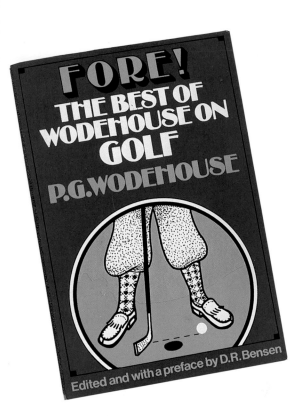

## THE GOLF COURSE

Geoffrey S. Cornish, Ronald E. Whitten (Rutledge, 1987)

This encyclopedic tome traces the history of golfing terrain, along with the architects who laid out the courses we play on. *The Golf Course* is a comprehensive reference for checking out the provenance of over 10,000 courses worldwide; included also are biographical profiles of just about every man who ever designed a course.

## THE BOGEY MAN

George Plimpton (Harper & Row, 1967)

Plimton's bouts of participatory journalism are legion to Walter Mitteyesque sports fans everywhere. Here the author relates the treats and trials of a month of playing big-time golf with the pros. In addition to his actual experiences, the book delves into the lingo and lore of the golf tour. With Plimpton's characteristic humility and temporary-insider observations, *The Bogey Man* is a birdie read.

## FORE!
## THE BEST OF WODEHOUSE ON GOLF

(Ticknor & Fields, 1987)

If you're an avid reader and golf nut, and you've somehow missed P. G. Wodehouse, you're in for a treat. Set against the backdrop of a starchy British club, these marvelous short stories reveal the master satirist's appreciation for the obsessive nature of the game. Bitten by the golf bug at an early age, Wodehouse often lamented that he might have stood a better chance of getting his handicap down under eighteen had he spent more time on the game and less "fooling about writing stories and things."

## CONFESSIONS OF A HOOKER

Bob Hope, Dwayne Netland (Doubleday, 1987)

With quips on ex-presidents Ford, Ike and J.F.K., fellow-comedians Jackie Gleason, Bing Crosby and Jack Benny, pros Walter Hagen, Ben Hogan and Arnold Palmer, Bob Hope successfully threads golf, humor and politics. An endless stream of one-liners makes the material strikingly similar to a Hope monologue, but his lifelong love affair with the game is never compromised.

# THE BOOK OF GOLF DISASTERS

Peter Dobereiner (Perennial, 1983)

Golfers worldwide stand united by the dark cloud of ignominy that hangs overhead at one time or another. Dobereiner brings cheer to all by irreverently recalling some of the most outrageous incidents, such as DeVicenzo losing the Masters by signing the wrong scorecard, Sam Snead's run-in with an ostrich or Byron Nelson losing a tourney when his caddie accidentally kicked his ball.

# THE NEW RULES OF GOLF

Tom Watson with Frank Hannigan (Random House, 1984)

Most golfers would probably claim little need for such a book, but the sad fact is, over ninety percent need it. Like most pros, Watson is a lifelong stickler to the rules. Here he explains in common language the boundaries of the game. This guide is thoroughly comprehensive yet lively, with career anecdotes and illustrations. The message is clear: Learning the rules will help us all appreciate the game more.

# GOLF IN THE MAKING

Ian T. Henderson and David I. Stirk (Henderson and Stirk, 1979)

This handsome tome is expensive ($75) and found only in England or at Abercrombie & Fitch. But for those interested in the evolution of golf equipment it's a most fascinating reference manual—actually a history of the game—and a must for collectors.

# DEAD SOLID PERFECT

Dan Jenkins (Price Stern Sloan, 1986)

Dan Jenkins is the master at behind-the-scenes sports fiction *(Semi-Tough)*, and in this case professional golf takes it on the nose. It's a shame that the pro tour doesn't have the characters this book has, but that's literary license. Unlike pro golf, this fun read is breezy and raunchy.

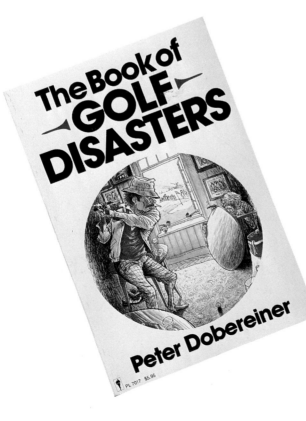

# GOLF VIDEOS

It's hard to believe that only ten years ago Jack Nicklaus came out with the first golf video: an eighteen-minute, one-camera exhibition on how to warm up for a round. Today, there are hundreds of titles available and more being released every day.

Book sections in pro shops are rapidly ceding space to the video selections, which shouldn't surprise McCluhanites ("The medium is the message") but may send a message to Jane Fonda. With over 1.5 million sold, golf videos pose a serious threat to front-running exercise tapes. It also shouldn't surprise that golfers might rather play golf than read about it, but when you can just slip a tape into the VCR and *see* how it should be done, the written word in golfland is in serious trouble.

Selecting instructional tapes from the superabundance of choice is a slight bit more complex than deciding between a 7- or an 8-iron and a slight bit more expensive ($30 to $90). Video stores usually have a few titles for rent; libraries lend some, as well. Best bet may be to pass the hat around and co-purchase a few with some friends.

The golf videos surveyed here are some of the best available, both for informational value and quality of presentation. They may not be as much fun as *Star Wars,* but if they can lower your score . . . why not?

# GOLF DIGEST SCHOOLS LEARNING LIBRARY SERIES

(26 minutes each)

The Golf Digest Schools now have a customized learning program, whereby you work on specific parts of the game. With a choice of ten different tapes, you can just about cover all aspects of the game. As for the instructors, there are few if any equals to Bob Toski, Jim Flick, Davis Love, et al. Each twenty-six-minute tape costs thirty dollars—about the price of an average private lesson. The tapes:

    Vol. 1: A Swing for a Lifetime
    Vol. 2: Find Your Own Fundamentals
    Vol. 3: Driving for Distance
    Vol. 4: Sharpen Your Short Irons
    Vol. 5: Saving Par from the Sand
    Vol. 6: Putting for Profit
    Vol. 7: When the Chips Are Down
    Vol. 8: Winning Pitch Shots
    Vol. 9: Hitting the Long Shots
    Vol. 10: Trouble Shots: The Great Escapes

# SYBERVISION

Al Geiberger, Patty Sheehan (60 minutes each)

The idea behind "Sybervision" video-golf is to take the film image of the golf swing and have it trigger a sensation of movement in the viewer. The process is something called neuromuscular programming, and is presented in a series of graceful camera angles of model swings, accompanied by music. There is no talking, no verbal instructions. Ultimately, repeated viewings will enable the mind to retain a clear sensory image of ideal skill—theoretically.

There are two main Sybervision tapes, Men's Golf (Al Geiberger) and Women's Golf (Patty Sheehan); both "models" were chosen for their ideal swing mechanics and tempo. The creators of the system stress following the accompanying training guide, a manual fraught with terms such as biomechanical reinforcement, computer-enhanced movement, lower-body focus and more. Recommended for the highly imaginative golfer.

# BOB TOSKI TEACHES YOU GOLF

GD/T (56 minutes)

One of the game's great teachers, the diminutive Toski (you don't need size to play the game—or to hit the ball far, for that matter) discloses his methods in condensed form. The tape is divided (and subdivided) into three parts: (1) On the Green, (2) Around the Green and (3) Tee to Green.

# THE ART OF PUTTING

Ben Crenshaw (44 minutes), HDG

Long acknowledged as the best pure putter around, Ben Crenshaw here gives a simple and direct, step-by-step private putting lesson. All the essentials are covered: grip, stance, feel, stroke (long and short), reading greens and warming up. Ever the golf historian, he uses a selection of old film clips to analyze the putting strokes of legendary champions of the past.

# BETTER GOLF NOW!

Ken Venturi (40 minutes), HPG

Ken Venturi is probably better known for his golf tips on TV than his fine record as a pro. No problem. Through the use of excellent mental images (e.g. pistol, paintbrush and fishing rod) he uses this same entertaining style to walk the golfer through fundamentals from tee to green. Near the end, a ''mini-lesson'' reviews key points.

# BOBBY JONES: HOW I PLAY GOLF

Sybervision (180 minutes)

This is the new king of golf video and the price reflects it—$250 for two tapes and a book on Jones' life. The tapes come in a series of eighteen golf lessons, which were filmed by Warner Brothers from 1931 to 1933, at a cost of one million dollars, a scary sum at the time.

Jones was a great teacher, and on film he had the natural presence of a studio leading man. The lessons cover every facet of golf and are each presented within the framework of vignettes, featuring such stars as W. C. Fields, James Cagney, Edward G. Robinson, Loretta Young, Joan Blondell and Douglas Fairbanks, Jr. If the plots are sometimes weak and silly, they are all saved by the magnificent Jones and his effortless, perfect swing. The camera work and special effects are quite advanced and artistic, but overall it's Jones' magnificent articulation of technique and fundamentals that is so striking. You step back in time, you sit back and watch, and you marvel at the most perfect swing you'll ever see, implemented with what, compared to today, is antiquated equipment.

# GOLF MY WAY

Jack Nicklaus (128 minutes), Worldvision

All right, so Jack Nicklaus will never be confused with Jack Nicholson. But what he lacks in showmanship he makes up for with a forthright style and an honest desire to impart his unparalleled wealth of golf knowledge. *Golf My Way* includes loads of action and golf shots, buffered by thorough instruction from the master. Excellent graphics make it easy to follow, and the Golden Bear's powerful and dynamic swing is a constant source of inspiration. Now if they only didn't have that silly, dinky musical refrain that annoyingly pops up every few frames.

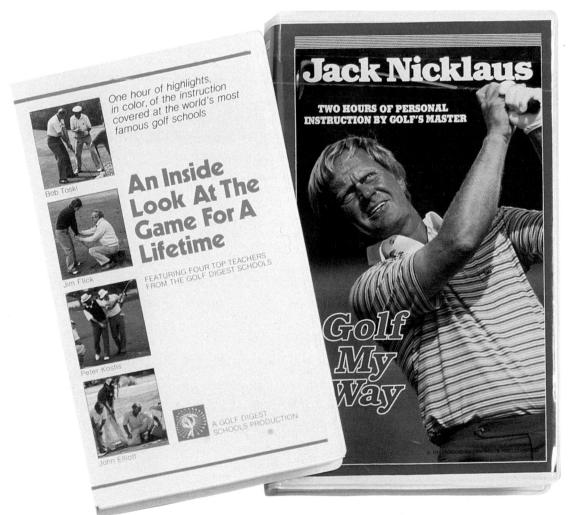

# EXERCISES FOR BETTER GOLF

Dr. Frank Jobe (73 minutes), PGA

Too many golfers ride in electric cars and play the game without any concern for physical improvements. Too many golfers injure themselves for lack of warming up and stretching. This exercise program—based on research from Centinela Hospital's Biomechanics Lab—is geared toward strengthening golf muscles, increasing flexibility, developing endurance and lowering the risk of injury.

# KEYS TO GREAT GOLF

JoAnne Carner (90 minutes), Nova Productions

JoAnne Carner has always been the longest of the hitters on the ladies tour, and on this tape she strives to help everyone hit the ball farther than ever before. With contagious enthusiasm, Carner demonstrates "little and not-so-little trade secrets" for all parts of the game. Highly recommended for both men and women—with the possible exception of the section aimed at the "Dolly Partons of golf."

# GOLF FOR KIDS OF ALL AGES

Wally Armstrong (50 minutes), Gator

Aided by Gabby the animated gator, Wally Armstrong and his son Scott entertainingly teach the fundamentals. This tape truly is for kids; it's a guaranteed good-time viewing, and it's a good bet they'll learn some golf.

# HOW TO GOLF

Jan Stephenson (50 minutes), Lorimar

Primarily for beginners, this video teaches intelligently by showing, analyzing and correcting the swings of novices. Color-coded references help the viewer work on specific aspects of the game, and Ms. Stephenson's naturally attractive mien only enhances the fast-paced package.

# GOLF SCHOOLS

A group of hopeful hackers working on their chipping at Ben Sutton.

One of the most difficult things for a golfer to admit is that his overall well-being might benefit from the golf-school experience. Cost aside, the idea of spending a few days, even weeks, restructuring the swing by hitting hours upon hours of balls off a practice tee is humbling and even downright scary.

To their credit, more and more hackers are seeking out this form of higher education. Of course, most schools offer a vacation-like atmosphere of swimming pools, cocktail parties and prizes to ease the pain.

Today, golf schools have become big business, as instruction is now combined with getaway vacations. Prices vary anywhere from $200 to $3,000, depending on the length of your stay, type of instruction and accommodations. Here's a brief listing of ten well-established, reputable schools, along with some of their features.

**BEN SUTTON GOLF SCHOOLS**
(Sun City Country Club, Florida)
P.O. Box 9199
Canton, OH 44711
(800) 225-6923
Features: seven-to-one student/teacher ratio, nine-hole practice course, video analysis, graph-check sequence pictures, unlimited daily golf after school.

**JOHN JACOBS' PRACTICAL GOLF SCHOOLS**
(Arizona, Florida, California, Hawaii, Colorado, Michigan and Scotland)
7127 East Sahuaro
Suite 101
Scottsdale, AZ 85254
(800) 472-5007
Features: eight-to-one maximum student/teacher ratio, attendance by world-renowned instructor Jacobs, variety of practice, some on-course instruction (actual playing-round lesson).

**BERTHOLY METHOD GOLF SCHOOLS**
Foxfire G & CC
Jackson Springs, N.C. 27281
(919) 281-3093
Features: two-to-one student/teacher ratio, six-student limit, indoor-outdoor complex, learn teaching positions before motions, patented swing-pipe training device.

**GOLF DIGEST INSTRUCTION SCHOOLS**
(Florida, California, Alabama, Georgia, Massachusetts, New York, Illinois, Ohio, Idaho, Hawaii, the Bahamas)
5520 Park Avenue
Box 395
Trumbull, CT 06611
(800) 243-6121
Features: seven-to-one maximum student/teacher ratio, choose from top training staff (Runyan, Love, Toski, Flick, Kostis), ten different types of schools, handicap placing, personal drills, take-home video.

## CRAFT-ZAVICHAS GOLF SCHOOL
(Arizona, California, North Carolina, South Carolina, Colorado)
600 Dittmer Avenue
Pueblo, CO 81005
(303) 564-4449
Features: six-to-one maximum student/teacher ratio, use custom-fitted Ping clubs, video analysis with stop action, graph-check camera, a special device shows club-face opening-closing, free range balls and greens fees.

## JERI REID'S GOLF SCHOOL
2059 Southwest 15th Street
Deerfield Beach, FL 33442
(305) 429-0623
Features: four-to-one maximum student/teacher ratio, instruction primarily for women (schools available for couples), unlimited golf, power-swing device, classroom psychology sessions, chipping board.

Courtesy Ben Sutton Golf School

## JIMMY BALLARD GOLF WORKSHOP
Doral Country Club
4400 N.W. 87th Ave.
Miami, FL 33178
(305) 592-2000
Five-to-one maximum student/teacher ratio, take-home video with review and comments by Ballard (world-famous teacher), all instructors have worked with Ballard for at least five years.

## JACK NICKLAUS ACADEMY OF GOLF
Grand Cypress Resort
One North Jacaranda
Orlando, FL 32819
(800) 835-7377
Features: seven-to-one maximum student/teacher ratio, "model" P.G.A. golfer to fit each student's physical characteristics, take-home video, academy notebook, computerized club fitting, on-course instruction.

## THE STRATTON GOLF SCHOOL
Stratton Mountain, VT 05155
(800) 843-6867
Features: five-to-one student/teacher ratio, playing lesson, twenty-two acre practice facility, putting computer, video analysis, unlimited free golf.

## THE GOLF CLINIC AT PEBBLE BEACH
P.O. Box M
Carmel, CA 93921
(800) 821-1586
Features: six-to-one maximum student/teacher ratio, video analysis with instructor's personalized commentary, club-head speed and direction measured, on-course instruction at Pebble Beach and Spyglass courses, special tour-professional-appearance weeks available.

# *SWING ANALYZERS*

Used to be, swing analysis was limited to the comments of the golf pro on the practice tee. Today, computers will tell you, or him, what you're doing wrong and how to correct. High technology has become an integral part of the teaching process; few golf schools are without computers. The idea is to tell the golfer more than if he's just hitting into a net—they even help with club-fitting. If there's anything keeping teaching pros around—aside from the personal touch that some of us still prefer—it's the price of these damn things. But who ever said golf was cheap, anyway?

## GOLFTEK

The first computer-swing analyzer, Golftek was designed in 1976 by Bud Blankenship, an engineer who fled Silicon Valley. His latest model, the Pro III, measures carry, club-head speed, swing path, tempo, shape of the shot and point of impact on the club-face. The Pro III can also hook up to a monitor, showing a color-graphics reproduction of golf terrain. The hit is superimposed, showing where the ball landed and how far off the tee.

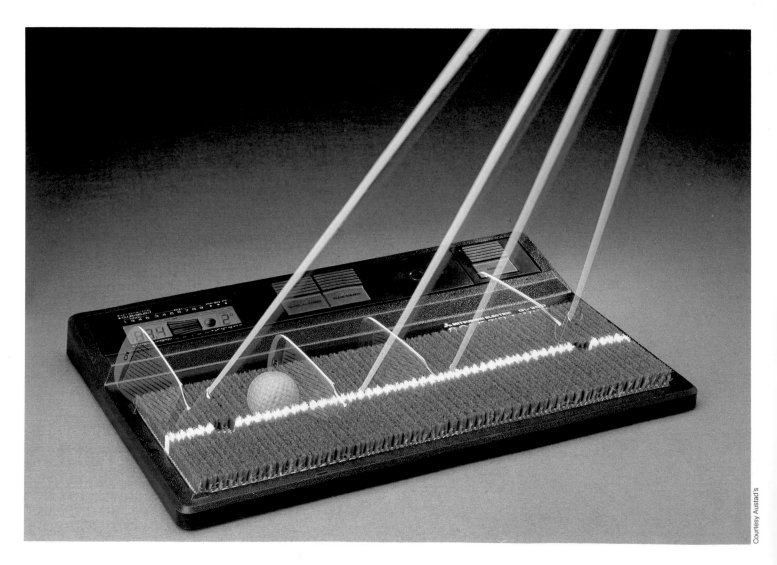

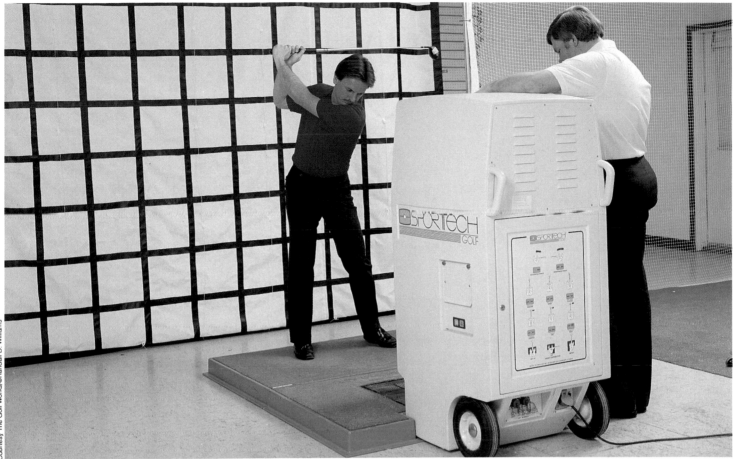

Courtesy The Golf Works/©Randall D. Williams

# MATT

The state of the art in swing computers, MATT (Motion Analysis Teaching Technology) is a million-dollar machine that produces three-dimensional views of a golfer's swing in the most minute detail. The golfer has to suit up in vest and straps with lightweight sensors while three different camera angles record the swing. Trouble spots are then located through the computer's wealth of data—hips, hands, even a finger can be pinpointed, allowing the golfer to pinpoint aspects of the swing he's never seen before. The images are stored and can later be recalled to be compared and checked for improvement.

# SPORTECH

The Sportech Swing Analyzer looks like a video game, which in a sense it is. After you've stepped onto the mat and hit the ball into a net a few feet away, fifty-five light sensors will have measured your club-head speed, face angle and impact position, and backswing-downswing paths. Special scales under your feet calculate the amount of weight distribution at setup, top of swing and impact. The monitor and/or a printout now gives you all the vital stats. Here's where the golf pro comes in—hopefully he can translate this info into a reading of your shortcomings. Otherwise, you're both stuck with a page of Chinese algebra.

# MITSUBISHI

The budget item in computer golf right now (under $200), Mitsubishi's Golf Trainer serves as a home practice unit (provided you have a good net). It's also less complex (fewer sensors) and provides less detailed information. It will give you club-head speed and face angle, distance, and an "out of bounds" reading if the ball "lands" more than forty-four yards off line. Also works for putting, measuring direction, face angle and head speed.

*Opposite page:* The Mitsubishi swing analyzer is the budget home-practice version of the large machines some golf schools use. *Above:* Sportech, the state of the art of swing analyzers. Bring along a pro to interpret the data.

# DRIVING RANGES

*"What a shame to waste those great shots on the practice tee. I'd be afraid of finding out what I was doing wrong."*
—Walter Hagen

Like many of the pros of his day, Walter Hagen hated to practice. Today, it's a different story; you just don't get good without putting your time in at the range—or the practice tees, as they're referred to at country clubs.

**Maniac Hill,** the first driving range in America, still serves the seven courses at Pinehurst. It is also one of the more elegant ranges you'll see, with its four tiers used alternately to let the grass regrow. Most ranges today don't have grass, offering Astroturf mats instead, from which getting the ball airborne can be quite difficult.

With the price of metropolitan real estate, the driving range in some big cities is rapidly nearing extinction. The indoor bubble ranges of the seventies were for some reason a bust, while today more and more water ranges are cropping up. The floating balls in use only sacrifice ten percent of distance, indicated by markers on buoys.

But the real range troopers are the Japanese. The golf craze rages on over there, despite the fact that, due to supply and demand, most hackers may not get to a course for years. For them the range is the only game in town, even with three-hour waits. Triple-decked ranges are not uncommon, and one place in downtown Tokyo has customers hitting into a net that extends over a crowded street. (The balls roll back.) Some boat cruises even offer knocking balls toward a floating "green" barge that is towed a hundred yards behind.

If you'd like to go into the range business, you need look no farther than the **Eastern Golf Corporation** (telephone: (800) 482-7200). Other than land, they offer everything you need: range balls, range clubs, tee mats, rule signs (No Horseplay Allowed), custom cages, specialized netting, ball painters, ball dispensers, range "sweep" ball pickers and hard hats.

Keith Glasgow

# MUSEUMS

There are two golf museums on the East Coast to appeal to more than just the historically curious. The U.S.G.A.'s **Golf House,** in Far Hills, N.J., is a beautiful Colonial-style mansion which houses an intricate maze of room-by-room displays that include (among other things): clubs and balls as they've evolved through the ages; the golf club used on the moon; photographs, paintings and videos of the greats; a signed scorecard from J.F.K.; clubs of champions; changing golf fashions; a library with over 7,000 golf books. The P.G.A.'s **World Golf Hall of Fame,** in Pinehurst, N.C., includes many of the same type of artifacts as Golf House, if less bountiful. Highlights: a golf-ball slot machine; Al Geiberger's scorecard for his record fifty-nine, an amazing, artistically arranged pencil collection from eighty percent of the nation's courses; and antique clubs used by "Old" and "Young" Tom Morris to win their eight British Open titles in the 1860s and 1870s.

*Above:* A typical covered range in New Jersey, where the hordes can hack away, rain or shine. *Left:* An old golf ball slot machine in the Golf House Museum, Far Hills, New Jersey.

*Opposite left:*
Ben Hogan
hated to teach,
but you could
learn by just
watching his
swing (or reading
his books).
*Opposite right:*
Bob Toski, the
Mighty Mouse,
is widely
recognized as one
of the world's top
teachers.

# TEACHING PROS

It's a generally accepted golf maxim that playing pros make lousy teaching pros. Some actually don't know why they hit the ball so well, others can't articulate it. Many simply don't care to give up hard-gained know-how. Ben Hogan hated to teach, even if he did co-write one of the greatest golf texts ever *(Five Lessons)*. Sam Snead once refused to give a golfer advice, explaining, "I gamble against you too much."

Conversely, the great golf educators spend more time watching and theorizing than playing. What they're able to see, they parlay into helping others—bless them. Some teaching pros are born after failed stints on the tour, but the great ones know their calling early on. Five of the very best ever:

## ERNEST JONES

Jones probably would have had a playing career but for losing a leg in World War I. (He shot an eighty-three on the day he left the hospital.) In the 1940s he opened the first indoor golf school in New York City, where he first promoted his famous "swing the club head" theme. By this he meant a pure swinging action with the hands, letting the body follow the lead—without fighting centrifugal force. To demonstrate he used a pocketknife tied to a handerchief. By swinging the hands the knife follows naturally. Many contemporary pros teach his theories, most of which are based on keeping a simple outlook toward the game.

## JIMMY BALLARD

If Jimmy Ballard is just now starting to get the respect he deserves, it's because the professionals he's helped aren't generous in doling out credit to his dynamic style. Ballard apprenticed at a driving range under former major-leaguer Sam Byrd, who credited Babe Ruth's hitting for some of his golf tenets. Ballard has refined Byrd's theories based on the idea of "connection"—that swinging is a coordinated movement of the entire body, with the big muscles of the upper body and legs leading the smaller muscles of the arms and hands. To get the feeling, he suggests the underhand throwing of a medicine ball, though lately he extols Bobby Knight's throwing a chair at a referee as the perfect golf-swing image.

## BOB TOSKI

When he was the leading money-winner and smallest player on the golf tour in 1954, Bob Toski was known as "Mouse," then "Mighty Mouse." He retired a few years later to the instruction tee and has since become "Dr. Swing," the most sought-after teacher in America. As dean and founder of the Golf Digest Schools, his methods are varied and well rounded, and always clear and graspable. "Powerless effort, not effortless power," he stresses. "Let the ball get in the way of the club." While Toski doesn't charge fellow-pros for advice, he more than makes up for it with his lay pupils, who he likes to say are better off paying him than a psychiatrist.

©USGA Golf House

©USGA Golf House

## ALEX MORRISON

Alex Morrison began as a caddie in 1908 at the L.A. Country Club, where he would eventually become head professional. In high school, he learned anatomy and photography, the better to dissect the golf swing, the study of which would occupy his entire life. In a less serious vein, Morrison traveled the vaudeville circuit in the twenties and thirties, explaining his swing theory, performing trick shots and whacking cotton balls into the audience. His most adamant teachings—imparted mostly on Hollywood's finest— insisted on "left-side dominance," by which maximum force was transmitted through the left shoulder and arm to the club.

## HARVEY PENNICK

All his life, Harvey Pennick has cured ailing swings by teaching fundamentals rather than any method. In his eighties now, he still keeps an eye on the practice range at Austin Country Club, where he was head pro for half a century. (He began caddying there around the Civil War and never left.) Pennick's reputation among pros lies in his adaptability. "People are different—not everyone's hands can look the same on a club," he says. Because of this outlook, his personal perceptions have drawn the greatest of pros over the years. "I teach players to stick with their natural tendencies." Good players, of course.

# MISCELLANEOUS AIDS

Thankfully, there are various ways to while the time away off the course; all of them, naturally, involve hitting a golf ball. We suggest these affordable obsessive training gadgets (from Austads mail order telephone: (800) 843-6828)—guaranteed to keep you happy and to drive your loved ones nuts).

The **Practice Net,** measuring seven feet by nine feet, can be set up just about anywhere. Framed within steel tubing, the nylon netting stops shots on impact, and a smaller backup net keeps balls from rolling. Also available is the accompanying nonsliding **Driving Mat** with rubber tee and thick Astroturf.

The **Chip-N-Pitch Net,** with its twenty-four-inch-diameter hoop, is an ideal practice aid for the short game.

The nine-foot indoor **Putting Green** is the classic office time-waster. A foam incline near the hole provides a gradual rise; a backstop catches near misses.

The eight-foot-square **Target Mat** creates an imaginary green—albeit a small one—for finesse shots. Comes with six-foot pin flag.

Courtesy Hammacher Schlemmer

*Opposite page:* A practice net for backyard chipping helps make any hacker more accurate. *Left:* Nine-foot indoor putting green, for office time-wasters. *Below:* Practice net with target.

Courtesy Austad's

SECTION IV
*Goofy Golf*

*Right:* Combination serious-gag score sheet for the 19th hole. *Opposite page:* Snow golfers, a growing contingent—some people will play golf anywhere, anytime.

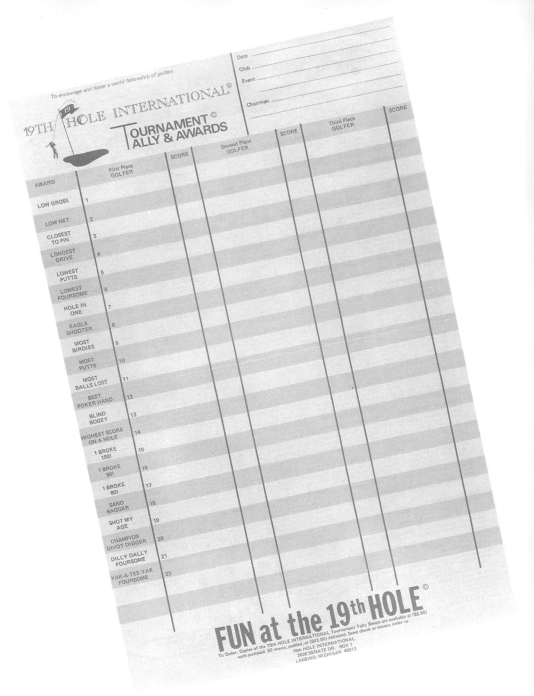

# ODD COMPETITIONS

## ICE FOLLIES

Played over frozen Nesmith Lake outside Akron, Ohio every February, the **Chili Open** (named for the cauldrons of hot stuff served) attracts hundreds of entries annually. Snowplows clear the "fairways," Astroturf is placed on the "greens," and the cups are groomed with an ice augur. Snow "traps" were added when shrewd competitors tried rolling the ball down the ice; since then, only top-wedge players succeed. In 1984, 800 entrants watched the ice melt as temps hit the fifties. A hole-in-one contest was held along the muddy banks, but no one scored an ace.

The annual **Golf-in-the-Snow Tournament** in St. Paul, Minnesota, is somehow played in snows that average between 1½ and 3 feet in depth. No penalties for lost ball, nor for missed hits, since it's so easy to hit under the ball. The object is to hit a cup on each green, ten feet in diameter and marked with blue spray paint. Most players lose between ten and fifteen balls. There is no putting—how could anyone putt?

## DOUBLE TROUBLE

Tough to tell the players apart at the 1986 Double Trouble Golf Tournament, a fund-raiser for the Twins Foundation. Nine sets of identical twins showed up at the Chanute Country Club, in Chanute, Kansas and it's presumed they all shot their own shots. Matched twosomes, anyone?

## BOBBY JONES OPEN

What's in a name? In the case of the **Bobby Jones Open,** held annually in the Detroit suburbs, the right name earns you the right to enter, only it has to be Robert Jones.

The Open is the brainchild of a computer programmer named, what else, Robert Jones. Jones loved golf and thought "other golf-playing Bob Joneses would like to get together and see what we all looked like." So in 1979 he scoured area phone books and eventually fed a master list of 300 B.J.s into his computer. In 1984, the field included sixty-five fat, skinny, short, tall, young and old B.J.s, ranging in profession from banker to songwriter to contractor to priest. With a few introductions, most players carry such monikers as Banker Bob, Kleenex Bob, Orchestra Bob and No-Sag Bob, the winner of the first two competitions. First prize is a trip to Atlanta, home of the Bobby Jones who might be turning in his grave.

## COWPATCH OPEN

For seven straight years, they've held the **Booneville Open Cow Pasture Golf Tournament** at Newton Davis's 170-acre cow pasture in Arkansas. The idea is to eventually raise enough money for a golf course for Booneville. Barbed wire marks out-of-bounds and meadow muffins abound, but the cows are removed a week earlier so that the "course" is "dry" by the time play starts. Hopefully one day they'll have their course.

*Right:* A member of the Laid Back Golfer's Association (LBGA) models the ultimate in unnecessary footwear: beach thongs with cleats. *Above right:* Seeing double? Three twosomes from the 1986 Double Trouble tournament.

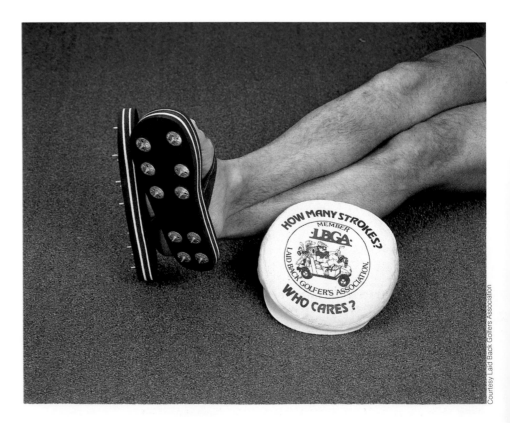

# LAID BACK

"We believe you can enjoy the great game of golf without taking it so seriously," says Max Colclasure, founder of the Laid Back Golfers Association, an organization dedicated to fighting high blood pressure. In 1987, the L.B.G.A. drew 100 players who obviously feel the same way to the second annual **Mulligan Classic** in Las Vegas. ("No lying, no cheating, and no sandbagging necessary, because your golf score, fact or fiction, doesn't mean a flip.") Who won? Who cares?

# AMERICA'S WORST GOLFER

Angelo Spagnolo may not yet be a household name, but his career is still young. In 1985, he officially became the worst golfer in America.

Why on earth the sedate and austere P.G.A. would sanction such a goofy event as the **Worst Avid Golfer** on their showcase course at Sawgrass is anybody's guess. Maybe they want to cater to the hacker in all of us.

Spagnolo's winning effort was insured when he scored a sixty-six on the treacherous seventeenth, a par-three island hole, famous for its inviting water hazard. He deposited twenty-seven balls into the drink before choosing to putt his way up the peninsular cartway path. The duffer supreme finished with a twenty-two at the eighteenth for a total of 257. Bear in mind that all four participants—chosen from 627 nominees—play regularly and were actually trying their best. They're simply that bad.

*Below:* Roberto DeVincenzo, remembered as the man who signed the wrong scorecard at the Masters. *Right:* Tommy "Thunder" Bolt, he of the terrible temper and the smooth swing. *Opposite page:* A young DeVicenzo at the 1950 British Open.

# BAD BOYS, GIRLS AND GOOFY GREATS— TEN BEST

**MAC O'GRADY** plays right-handed, putts left-handed, runs in marathons, speaks Japanese, likes to talk about Isaac Newton's influence on golf and loves to rock the boat. He spent twelve years trying to make the P.G.A. Tour. Once there, he spent the next four waging war against the ruling powers over a $500 fine for calling a volunteer a "bitch."

**TOMMY "THUNDER" BOLT,** one of golf's original bad boys, is most remembered for flinging his driver into the lake at Cherry Hills at the 1960 U.S. Open. Bolt's silky-smooth swing was overshadowed by a reputation for tantrums that was largely unjustified and greatly exaggerated. But after such incident, where he had snapped a shaft in two against a fence, he confronted a reporter saying the scribe should have "checked and made sure the heat and humidity hadn't made my grips slick."

©Bob Daemmrich

©Bob Daemmrich

**JIM KING** was fined and suspended for cursing and choking an official who stood in his putting line at a tournament in 1973. The former college football player and armed-forces boxer today sourly continues to march to the beat of his own drum on the Senior Tour.

**ROBERTO DEVICENZO,** one of the all-time greats, is most fondly remembered for a tournament he lost: the 1968 Masters. In total strokes, the Argentinean actually tied Bob Goalby, but the playoff was canceled when it was discovered that he had actually given himself an incorrect 4 rather than 3 on the seventy-first hole. According to the rules, the score had to stand, and the gaffee dropped DeVicenzo to second.

*Below:* Jan Stephenson, arguably golf's bad girl, unarguably one of the greatest women ever to lift a club. *Right:* The quintessential gamesman, Walter Hagen.

**JANE BLALOCK** was accused in 1972 by her peers of cheating by mismarking her ball to advantage before putting. The militant golfer was the wrong person to accuse without evidence. After a suspension and fine from the L.P.G.A., she was reinstated after an appeals court ruled in her favor and ordered reimbursement to the tune of $100,000.

**RICK MEISSNER** couldn't make a cent on the Tour during the 1977–78 season, but you gotta pay the rent, especially if you have no sponsor. After an initial conviction, Meissner confessed to having robbed a total of nineteen Maryland banks of nearly $100,000 during his fruitless playing days.

**JUMBO OZAKI'S** 1988 Master's invitation was rescinded when it was discovered through a Japanese newspaper's exposé that he had associated with members of a crime syndicate. All he'd really done was play in a few corporate outings with some shady characters. Has the entire Masters field always been that clean?

© Britt Laughlin/ BMA–The Photo Source

**JAN STEPHENSON'S** quasi-pornographic photo layouts incurred the wrath of her fellow touring pros, but never affected her scores. In fact, the confusing saga of her 1982 marriage-annulment-separation-divorce-property battle hardly affected her game either. Some might even say she's given women's golf a lift.

**DAVE HILL,** the most penalized and outspoken player in golf, is the game's answer to John McEnroe. Once, at the end of a particularly distasteful round and before a national TV audience, an official warned Hill not to break his putter. Too late. He snapped it in half, tapped his putt in with the broken-off head, and took a two-month suspension. In his 1977 opus *Teed Off*, Hill admitted starting off golf days with Benzedrine backed by vodka-orange-juice chasers.

**WALTER HAGEN** was, on the surface, the consummate gentleman, but opponents knew him as the ultimate gamesman and con artist, a master of the psych job. Before Hagen's day, talking on the tees was virtually taboo, until he introduced the subtle chatter that would unnerve his victims. When a fellow-reveler once told him in the wee hours that his opponent had long since gone to bed, Hagen answered, "He may be in bed, but he ain't sleeping."

# WHITE HOUSE GOLF

Among the most famous presidential linksmen were Warren Harding (*below*) and Dwight D. Eisenhower (*right*).

**William Howard Taft** used to make the members at Chevy Chase Country Club (Maryland) maintain a two-hole gap behind his foursome, which made him very unpopular. **Warren Harding** drank on the course during Prohibition. **Woodrow Wilson** was out golfing when informed the Lusitania had been sunk. (He didn't finish his round.)

   **Dwight Eisenhower** putted constantly over the Oval Office rugs. He also had a mini-course built at Camp David and had a green groomed on the South Lawn at the White House. When **John F. Kennedy** became president, one of the first things he noticed was a spike-worn path from the Office to the green. J.F.K. was supposedly an excellent golfer, though he played little and had a reputation for "picking up" short putts for "gimmes." No one argued.

**Lyndon Baines Johnson** liked to play holes out of order. Asked about L.B.J.'s swing, an aide responded, "Like he's killing snakes." And what did the Pres consider a gimme? "On the green." **Richard Nixon** eschewed the game, saying, "There are better things you can do with your time." **Gerald Ford** beaned a spectator with his first drive at a pro-am, then hit a policeman in a golf cart at the sixteenth hole. At another pro-am, **Spiro Agnew** hit his partner, professional Doug Sanders, from behind, opening a one-inch cut. At the same event the following year, Agnew hit three spectators with two shots. **Jimmy Carter** never played the game, but handed out signature-stamped souvenir balls. **Ronald Reagan** plays at least once a year, but his score is a state secret.

*Far left:* Spiro Agnew with Jackie Gleason at Inverarry, 1971. *Left:* Ronald Reagan. *Below:* Woodrow Wilson checking the distance on his drive.

©Pete Souza/The White House

©USGA Golf House

# BIBLIOGRAPHY

Braine, Tim and John Stravinsky. *The Not-So-Great-Moments in Sports.* New York: Quill, 1986.

Chieger, Bob and Pat Sullivan. *Inside Golf.* New York: Atheneum, 1985.

Brown, Gene. *The New York Times Encyclopedia of Sports, Vol. 5.* New York: Arno, 1975.

Cornish, Geoffrey S., and Ronald E. Whitten. *The Golf Course.* New York: Rutledge, 1987.

Henderson, Ian T., and David I. Stirk. *Golf in the Making.* Winchester, ENG: Henderson and Stirk Ltd., 1982.

Olman, John M., and Morton W. Olman. *The Encyclopedia of Golf Collectibles.* Florence, AL: Books Americana, 1985.

Plimpton, George. *The Bogey Man.* New York: Harper & Row, 1967.

Sheehan, Larry. *The Whole Golf Catalog.* New York: Atheneum, 1979.

Steel, Donald. *Golf Facts & Feats.* Middlesex, ENG: Guiness Superlatives Ltd., 1982

Viney, Laurence. *Benson and Hedges Golfer's Handbook.* London, ENG: Macmillan, 1986.

Wind, Herbert Warren. *Following Through.* New York: Ticknor & Fields, 1985.

# SOURCES

AltaPro Golf Inc.
4265 95th Street
Edmonton, Alberta T6E 5R6

Tommy Armour Golf
8350 North Lehigh Avenue
Morton Grove, IL 60053

Austads
4500 East 10th Street
Sioux Falls, SD 57196-1428

Browning Golf Co.
Route 1
Morgan, UT 84051

Ben Hogan Co.
2912 West Pafford Street
Fort Worth, TX 76109

The Booklegger
13100 Grass Valley Avenue
Grass Valley, CA 95945

Custom Golf Clubs Inc.
10206 North Interregional Hwy.
Austin, TX 78753

Eagles Only
*Distributed in Canada by:*
Robert Tate Sales Ltd.
Box 1370
Delta, British Columbia V4M 3Y8

Florida Golf Warehouse Inc.
4085D L.B. McLeod Road
Orlando, FL 32811

Foot-Joy Inc.
144 Field Street
Brockton, MA 02403-6009

The Golf Academy
T.G.A. Sports Enterprises Inc.
Suite 300 -1497 Marine Drive
West Vancouver, British Columbia
V7T 1B8

Mr. Golf
3112 East North Navarro
Victoria, TX 77901

The Golf Shopper
211 East Ocean Boulevard
Long Beach, CA 90802

The Golf Works
Ralph Maltby Enterprises
4820 Jacksontown Road
Newark, OH 43055-7199

Kangaroo Golf Motor Caddies
Highway 108 East Box 607
Columbus, NC 28722

Karsten Manufacturing Corporation
Ping Golf Clubs
2201 West Desert Cove
Phoenix, AZ 85068

Kenneth Smith Golf Clubs
Box 41901-G28
Kansas City, MO 64141

Lakewood Golf Cars
Box 159
Sylvan Lake, Alberta T0M 1Z0

Lefties Only
1972 Williston Rd.
South Burlington, VT 05403

MacGregor Golf Products
1601 South Slappey Blvd.
Albany, GA 31708

McCowan's Discount Golf Centre
4020 4th Street S.E.
Calgary, Alberta

Miller Golf's Tee House
R.R. 1
Hyde Park, Ontario

Mizuno Golf Co.
5805 Peachtreet Corners East
Norcross, GA 30092

Omnisport International Inc.
Corner Smith and Petrie Sts.
Box 730
St. Catharines, Ontario L2R 6Y6

Palm Springs Golf Co.
74-824 Lennon Place
Palm Desert, CA 92260

Pinseeker
3502 South Susan Street
Santa Ana, CA 92704

Powa-Kaddy
965 Central Avenue
St. Petersburg, FL 33705

Pro-Group Inc.
6201 Mountain View Rd.
Ooltewah, TN 37363

The Sharper Image
650 Davis Street
San Francisco, CA 94111

Slotline Golf
5252 McFadden Avenue
Huntington Beach, CA 92649

Spalding Sports Worldwide
425 Meadow Street
Chicopee, MA 01021-0901

Taylor Made Golf Company Inc.
2271 Cosmos Court
Carlsbad, CA 92008

Telepro Golf Shops
1425 North Main Street
Santa Ana, CA 927021-2320

Titleist Golf Co.
Belleville Avenue
Dept. A-3
New Bedford, MA 02741-0965

Edwin Watts Golf Shops
P.O. Box 1806
Fort Walton Beach, FL 32549

Wilson Sporting Goods
2233 West Street
River Grove, IL 60171

Yamaha Golf
P.O. Box 6600
Buena Park, CA 90620

Yonex Corporation
350 Maple Avenue
Torrance, CA 90503-2603

# INDEX

Anser putters, 44

Bags, 60-63
Balls, 50-59
  balancing device for, 76
  Cayman, 55
  as collectibles, 51
  colored, 59
  dimples on, 58
  Dunlop, 53
  Exploder, 56
  Floater, 56
  goof balls, 56
  Nitelite, 55
  Renegade, 56
  retrievers for, 79
  rules concerning, 54
  Spalding, 52
  storage device for, 79
Basakwerd putters, 49
Basket Retriever, 79
Books, 148-57
  *Art of Golf, The* (Simpson), 149
  *Bogey Man, The* (Plimpton), 156
  *Book of Golf Disasters, The* (Dobereiner), 157
  *Complete Golfer, The* (Vardon), 151
  *Confessions of a Hooker* (Hope and Netland), 156
  *Dead Solid Perfect* (Jenkins), 157
  *Down the Fairway* (Jones and Keeler), 150
  *Five Lessons* (Hogan and Wind), 152
  *Following Through* (Wind), 154
  *Fore! The Best of Wodehouse on Golf* (Wodehouse), 156
  *Getting Up and Down* (Watson), 151
  *Golf Begins at Forty* (Snead), 153
  *Golf Course, The* (Cornish and Whitten), 156
  *Golf in the Kingdom* (Murphy), 154
  *Golf in the Making* (Henderson and Stirk), 157
  *Green Road Home, The* (Bamberger), 155
  *How to Play Your Best Golf All the Time* (Armour), 150
  *Inner Game of Golf, The* (Gallwey), 153
  *On Learning Golf* (Boomer), 150
  *New Rules of Golf, The* (Watson), 157
  *New Way to Better Golf, A* (Morrison), 150
  *Nine Bad Shots of Golf, The (And What to Do about Them)* (Dante and Diegel), 151
  *Pigeons, Marks, Hustlers* (Snead), 154

*Play Better Golf* (Nicklaus), 153
*Play Great Golf* (Palmer), 149
*Search for the Perfect Golf Swing, The* (Cochran and Stobbs), 152
*Snake in the Sand Trap* (Trevino), 155
*Square-to-Square Golf Swing* (Aultman), 152
*Strokes of Genius* (Boswell), 154
*Teed Off* (Hill), 155
Browning pull-carts, 65
Bullseye putters, 46

Caddybag pull-carts, 66
Callaway Hickory Stick irons and woods, 24
Cash-in putters, 45
Cayman balls, 55
Check Go, 76
Clubs. *See* Irons and woods
Competitions, odd and unusual, 176-79
Computers, 34, 166-67
Country clubs
  Chicago Golf Club (Illinois), 109
  Glen Abbey (Ontario), 108
  Newport Country Club (Rhode Island), 108
  St. Andrews (New York), 106
  Shinnecock Hills (New York), 109
  The Country Club (Massachusetts), 106
  Toronto Golf Club (Ontario), 108
  *See also* Courses; Resorts
Courses—British Isles
  Ballybunion (Ireland), 98
  Carnoustie (Scotland), 136
  County Sligo (Ireland), 139
  Gleneagles (Scotland), 137
  Lahinch (Ireland), 140
  Muirfield (Scotland), 102
  Portmarnock (Ireland), 140
  Royal Birkdale (England), 134
  Royal County Down (Ireland), 102
  Royal Dornoch (Scotland), 136
  Royal Dublin (Ireland), 141
  Royal Lytham (England), 134
  Royal St. George (England), 135
  Royal Troon (Scotland), 137
  St. Andrews, (Scotland), 95
  St. Anne's (England), 134
  Sunningdale (England), 133
  Turnberry (Scotland), 138
  Walton Heath (England), 133
  Waterville (Ireland), 141
  *See also* Country clubs; Resorts
Courses—North America—private, 92-103
  Augusta National (Georgia), 97
  Oakmont (Pennsylvania), 98

Pebble Beach-Cypress Point (California), 101
Pine Valley (New Jersey), 97
Pinehurst Number 2 (North Carolina), 103
*See also* Country clubs; Resorts
Courses—North America—public and municipal
  Calgary (Alberta), 112
  Chicago (Illinois), 111
  Dallas (Texas), 112
  Detroit (Michigan), 113
  Edmonton (Alberta), 113
  Long Island (New York), 112
  Los Angeles (California), 113
  Milwaukee (Wisconsin), 112
  New York (New York), 113
  Phoenix (Arizona), 113
  San Diego (California), 113
  San Francisco (California), 111
  Toronto (Ontario), 112
  *See also* Country clubs; Resorts
Courses—other
  at airports, 145
  China, 145
  Eastern Europe, 145
  Kuwait, 142
  in prisons, 142
  in Third World countries, 145
  world's coldest, 142
  world's highest, 142
  *See also* Country clubs; Resorts

Dave Pelz putters, 45
Deluxe Ball Shagger, 79
Double Cup Retriever, 79
Driving mats, 172
Driving ranges, 168
Dunlop balls, 53

8802 putter, 46
Elmco golf cars, 71
Exploder ball, 56
EZ-GO golf cars, 69

Fashions, 81-89
Floater ball, 56
Foot-Joy gloves, 75

Gadgetry, 76-79
Gloves, 74-75
Golf cars, 69-71
Golftek swing analyzer, 166
Goofy Ball, 56

Highlander Company super stick, 36

Indoor practice devices, 172
Irons and woods, 13-41

Callaway Hickory Stick, 24
computer-aided design, 34
design categories, 41
diagram of, 19
fitting of, 18
fourteen-club rule, 27
glossary, 41
Highlander, 36
MacGregor, 30
moon club, 29
Northwestern Golf, 28
Orizaba Power Pod for, 33
Ping, 32
sand wedges, 38
shafts, 22
Slotline Inertial Chipper, 37
Spalding, 21
Stan Thompson Ginty, 27
Super Stick, 36
Taylor Made, 20
Tommy Armour, 18
True Temper, 37
Tycoon Graphite, 37
Wilson staff irons, 17
Yonex, 32
*See also* Putters

Kangaroo pull-carts, 65
Karsten Manufacturing. *See* Ping
Knickers, 87

MacGregor
    gloves, 75
    irons and woods, 30
    putters, 47
Matt swing analyzer, 167
Matzie putters, 49
Miller bags, 62
Mitsubishi swing analyzer, 167
Moon club, 29
Museums, 169

Nitelite balls, 55
Northwestern Golf irons and woods,
    28

Orizaba
    Power Pod, 33
    putters, 49

Pants, 87
Ping
    bags, 62
    irons and woods, 32
    putters, 44
Players, anecdotes, 180-83
Practice nets, 172
Presidents, U.S., 184-87
Pull-carts, 64-67
Putters, 43-49

Anser, 44
Basakwerd, 49
Bullseye, 46
Cash-in, 45
Dave Pelz, 45
8802, 46
MacGregor, 47
Matzie, 49
Orizaba, 49
Ping, 44
Ram Golf, 49
Response ZT, 47
Schenectady, 47
Slim Jim, 49
Spalding, 45
Titleist, 46
Wilson, 46
Zebra, 49
*See also* Irons and woods

Rainwear, 88
Ram Golf putters, 49
Rangefinder, 79
Renegade ball, 56
Resorts
    Alberta, 124
    Hawaii, 124-28
    Hilton Head (South Carolina),
        116-17
    Myrtle Beach (South Carolina),
        118-20
    Ontario, 129
    Palm Springs (California), 130-31
    Pinehurst (North Carolina), 123
    *See also* Country clubs; Courses
Response ZT putters, 47
Retrievers, 79

Sand wedges, 38
Schenectady putter, 47
Schools, 164-65
Shirts, 86
Shoes, 88
Slim Jim putters, 49
Slotline chipper, 37
Spalding
    balls, 52
    irons and woods, 21
Sportech swing analyzer, 167
Stan Thompson irons and woods,
    27
Swing analyzers, 166-67

Taylor Made irons and woods, 20
Teaching professionals, 170-71
Tees, 72-73
Titleist
    balls, 57
    putters, 46
Tommy Armour irons and woods,
    18

Trap-it Retriever, 79
True Temper shafts, 37
Tycoon Graphite irons and woods,
    37

Videotapes, 158-63
    *Art of Putting, The* (Crenshaw), 160
    *Better Golf Now!* (Venturi), 160
    *Bob Toski Teaches You Golf* (Toski),
        160
    *Bobby Jones: How I Play Golf* (Jones),
        161
    *Exercises for Better Golf* (Jobe), 162
    Golf Digest Schools Learning
        Library Series, 159
    *Golf for Kids of All Ages*
        (Armstrong), 162
    *Golf My Way* (Nicklaus), 161
    *How to Golf* (Stephenson), 162
    *Keys to Great Golf* (Carner), 162
    "Sybervision", 159

Wilson
    putters, 46
    Staff irons, 17
Woods. *See* Irons and woods

Yamaha golf cars, 71
Yonex irons and woods, 32

Zebra putters, 49

## Additional Photo Credits